The Australian Women's Weekly — Home Library

EDITOR: Maryanne Blacker

FOOD EDITOR: Pamela Clark

■ ■ ■

ART DIRECTOR: Sue de Guingand

DESIGNER: Robbylee Phelan

■ ■ ■

ASSISTANT FOOD EDITORS: Kathy Snowball,
Louise Patniotis

ASSOCIATE FOOD EDITOR: Enid Morrison

SENIOR HOME ECONOMISTS:
Kathy McGarry, Sophia Young

HOME ECONOMISTS: Frances Abdallaoui, Myles
Beaufort, Bronwen Clark, Caroline Jones, Leisel Rogers

EDITORIAL COORDINATOR: Elizabeth Hooper

KITCHEN ASSISTANT: Amy Wong

■ ■ ■

STYLISTS: Lucy Andrews, Wendy Berecry,
Marie-Helene Clauzon, Carolyn Fienberg, Jane Hann,
Rosemary de Santis

PHOTOGRAPHERS: Kevin Brown, Robert Clark,
Robert Taylor, Jon Waddy

■ ■ ■

HOME LIBRARY STAFF:

ASSISTANT EDITOR: Bridget van Tinteren

EDITORIAL COORDINATOR: Fiona Lambrou

■ ■ ■

ACP PUBLISHER: Richard Walsh

ACP DEPUTY PUBLISHER: Nick Chan

ACP CIRCULATION & MARKETING DIRECTOR:
Judy Kiernan

■ ■ ■

Produced by The Australian Women's Weekly Home Library.
Typeset by ACP Colour Graphics Pty Ltd. Colour separations
by Network Graphics Pty. Ltd. in Sydney. Printed by
Times Printers Pte Ltd, Singapore.
Published by ACP Publishing Pty. Limited,
54 Park Street, Sydney.
♦ AUSTRALIA: Distributed by Network Distribution Company,
54 Park Street Sydney, (02) 282 8777.
♦ UNITED KINGDOM: Distributed in the U.K. by Australian
Consolidated Press (UK) Ltd, 20 Galowhill Rd, Brackmills,
Northampton NN4 7EE (01604) 760 456.
♦ CANADA: Distributed in Canada by Whitecap
Books Ltd, 351 Lynn Ave, North Vancouver B.C.
V7J 2C4 (604) 980 9852.
♦ NEW ZEALAND: Distributed in New Zealand by Netlink
Distribution Company, 17B Hargreaves St, Level 5,
College Hill, Auckland 1 (9) 302 7616.
♦ SOUTH AFRICA: Distributed in South Africa by Intermag,
PO Box 57394, Springfield 2137 (011) 493 3200.

■ ■ ■

Potato Cookbook

Includes index.
ISBN 0 86396 027 9.

1. Cookery (Potatoes). I. Title: Australian
Women's Weekly. (Series: Australian
Women's Weekly Home Library).

641.6521

■ ■ ■

© A C P Publishing Pty. Limited
ACN 053 273 546
This publication is copyright. No part of it may be reproduced
or transmitted in any form without the written permission
of the publishers.
First printed 1994. Reprinted 1995

■ ■ ■

COVER: Clockwise from top right: Potato Rolls with Herbed
Bacon Filling, page 117, Sesame Potato Bread, page 116,
Spinach, Potato and Feta Cheese Pie, page 42, Crab and
Lemon Grass Double Crisps, page 24, Beetroot and Potato
Salad with Fresh Dates, page 67.
OPPOSITE: Best Ever Chips, page 86.
BACK COVER: From top: Kumara, Orange and Walnut
Doughnuts, Kumara Custards with Orange Cream,
Golden Kumara Waffles, page 113.

POTATO COOKBOOK

Potatoes are easily the world's most popular vegetable.
You can eat them every day – even in cakes, sweets and desserts –
and never tire of that luscious, satisfying taste. Make sure you
buy the right variety for the recipe. For example, potatoes with
a dry texture are generally best for frying (chipping),
whereas the moister potatoes are best for boiling. We help you
to know your potatoes on pages 120 and 121, but if you can't
obtain a particular variety, use one with similar qualities.
Our recipes specify old or new potatoes, or simply "potatoes",
in which case use an all-purpose variety.

Pamela Clark

FOOD EDITOR

*We would like to thank Dr A. W. Kellock, Industry Manager, Potatoes, Institute for Horticultural
Development, Toolangi, Victoria, for his help with this book.
We also thank Dobson's Potatoes, Acheron Valley Farms, Alexandra, Victoria;
J. C. Cut Bush and Co. of Dean, Victoria; and Franklins Big Fresh store at Leichhardt, NSW.*

BRITISH & NORTH AMERICAN READERS: Please note that
Australian cup and spoon measurements are metric. A quick conversion
guide appears on page 127.
A glossary explaining unfamiliar terms and ingredients appears on page 122.

Soups, Snacks & Starters

A well-dressed baked potato with a choice of tasty toppings is a treat that's hard to beat for popularity, but look further afield in this section and you'll find bags of fresh ideas and irresistible tastes to enjoy. The soups are winners – hot, thick and hearty, with textures ranging from creamy smooth and luscious, to chunky meals in a dish.

———————●———————

POTATO SOUP WITH TOMATO AND BASIL

30g butter
2 teaspoons olive oil
2 small (400g) leeks, chopped
2 cloves garlic, crushed
4 medium (800g) new potatoes, peeled, chopped
1 teaspoon grated lemon rind
2 bay leaves
1 litre (4 cups) vegetable stock

TOMATO TOPPING
1 tablespoon olive oil
1 small (200g) leek, finely chopped
1 clove garlic, crushed
2 large (500g) tomatoes, peeled, seeded, chopped
1 tablespoon chopped fresh basil

Heat butter and oil in pan, add leeks and garlic, cook, stirring, 3 minutes, cover, cook further 10 minutes or until leeks are soft. Add potatoes, rind, bay leaves and stock. Simmer, covered, about 20 minutes or until potatoes are tender. Push mixture through coarse sieve. Blend or process mixture in batches until smooth, serve with tomato topping.

Tomato Topping: Heat oil in pan, add leek and garlic, cook, covered, about 10 minutes or until leek is soft. Add tomatoes, cook, stirring occasionally, about 10 minutes or until mixture is thick. Stir in basil.

Serves 4.

- Recipe best made just before serving.
- Freeze: Not suitable.
- Microwave: Suitable.

POTATO AND BEAN SOUP WITH TOMATO PESTO

3 large (900g) potatoes, peeled, chopped
1.5 litres (6 cups) water
1 cup (150g) soup pasta
310g can red kidney beans, rinsed, drained
2 x 310g cans butter beans, rinsed, drained
¼ cup (20g) parmesan cheese flakes

TOMATO PESTO
2 medium (260g) tomatoes, peeled, seeded, chopped
1 cup firmly packed fresh basil leaves
2 cloves garlic, crushed
¼ cup (20g) grated parmesan cheese
¼ cup (60ml) olive oil

Combine potatoes and the water in pan, simmer, covered, about 25 minutes or until potatoes are just tender. Add pasta to potato mixture, simmer further 10 minutes or until pasta is just tender. Stir in beans, bring to boil, stir in tomato pesto. Serve with cheese flakes.

Tomato Pesto: Blend or process tomatoes, basil, garlic and cheese until smooth. Add oil gradually in a thin stream while motor is operating.

Serves 6 to 8.

- Recipe can be made a day ahead.
- Storage: Covered, in refrigerator.
- Freeze: Suitable.
- Microwave: Suitable.

RIGHT: From back: Potato and Bean Soup with Tomato Pesto, Potato Soup with Tomato and Basil.

China from Waterford Wedgwood.

SAMOSAS

1½ cups (225g) plain flour
30g butter
1 tablespoon poppy seeds
½ cup (125ml) warm water,
    approximately
vegetable oil for deep-frying

FILLING
1 medium (200g) potato, peeled
1 tablespoon vegetable oil
1 medium (150g) onion, chopped
1 clove garlic, crushed
2 teaspoons grated fresh ginger
1 teaspoon mild curry powder
1 teaspoon cumin seeds
1½ tablespoons chopped fresh mint
2 teaspoons lemon juice

Sift flour into bowl, rub in butter. Stir in seeds and enough water to form a firm dough. Knead dough on lightly floured surface about 5 minutes or until smooth; cover, refrigerate 30 minutes.

Roll dough on floured surface until 2mm thick. Cut into 8cm rounds. Spoon a level teaspoon of filling into centre of each round, lightly brush edges with water, fold over dough, using thumb and finger, pinch and fold over ends to seal.

Deep-fry samosas in batches in hot oil until browned, drain on absorbent paper. Serve hot.

Filling: Cut potato into 1cm cubes. Boil, steam or microwave potato until just tender. Heat oil in pan, add onion, garlic and ginger, cook, stirring, until onion is soft. Add curry powder and cumin seeds, cook, stirring, until fragrant. Stir in potatoes, mint and juice; cool 10 minutes.

Makes about 30.

- Uncooked samosas can be made a day ahead.
- Storage: Covered, in refrigerator.
- Freeze: Uncooked samosas suitable.
- Microwave: Potato suitable.

LEFT: Clockwise from top left: Garlic Potato Parcels with Dhal, Samosas, Moroccan Potato Triangles.

Setting from Grace Bros.

GARLIC POTATO PARCELS WITH DHAL

2 medium (400g) potatoes,
    peeled, chopped
1 clove garlic, crushed
1 tablespoon chopped fresh
    coriander
½ teaspoon ground cumin
½ teaspoon black mustard seeds
¼ teaspoon chilli powder
1 tablespoon lemon juice
1 egg yolk
2 teaspoons milk

PASTRY
1 cup (160g) wholemeal plain flour
½ cup (75g) white plain flour
1 teaspoon cumin seeds
50g butter
⅓ cup (80ml) water, approximately

DHAL
40g butter
1 medium (150g) onion, chopped
1 clove garlic, crushed
1 cup (200g) red lentils,
    washed, drained
2½ cups (625ml) hot water
1 teaspoon ground cumin
1 teaspoon garam masala
1 teaspoon ground turmeric

Boil, steam or microwave potatoes until tender, rinse under cold water; drain, mash. Combine mashed potato, garlic, coriander, cumin, seeds, chilli and juice in bowl; mix well. Roll pastry between sheets of baking paper until 2mm thick, cut out 20 x 10cm circles.

Place 1 tablespoon of potato mixture in centre of each pastry circle. Pinch pastry around mixture to seal. Place on greased oven trays, sealed side down, flatten slightly. Brush parcels with combined egg yolk and milk, make 3 small slits in top of each. Bake in moderately hot oven about 20 minutes or until browned. Serve potato parcels with dhal.

Pastry: Sift flours into bowl, add seeds, rub in butter (or process flours, seeds and butter until mixture resembles breadcrumbs). Add enough water to make ingredients cling together (or process until ingredients just come together). Press dough into a ball, knead gently on lightly floured surface until smooth. Wrap in plastic, refrigerate 30 minutes.

Dhal: Heat butter in pan, add onion and garlic, cook, stirring, until onion is soft. Add lentils, cook, stirring, further 2 minutes. Add water, simmer, covered, about 20 minutes or until lentils are soft. Stir in cumin, garam masala and turmeric.

Makes 20.

- Recipe can be prepared a day ahead.
- Storage: Covered, separately, in refrigerator.
- Freeze: Uncooked pastry suitable.
- Microwave: Potatoes and dhal suitable.

MOROCCAN POTATO TRIANGLES

2 large (600g) old potatoes
30g butter
1 tablespoon vegetable oil
1 medium (150g) onion, chopped
2 cloves garlic, crushed
2 teaspoons ground cumin
½ teaspoon ground fennel
¼ teaspoon chilli powder
2 teaspoons lemon juice
2 hard-boiled eggs, chopped
14 sheets fillo pastry
80g butter, melted, extra
2 teaspoons cumin seeds

Cook unpeeled potatoes on oven tray in moderately hot oven, about 1¼ hours or until tender. Cool potatoes 10 minutes, cut in half, scoop out flesh into bowl, add butter; mash well. Heat oil in pan, add onion and garlic, cook, stirring, until onion is soft; stir in spices, cook, stirring, until fragrant. Combine onion mixture with potato mixture, juice and eggs; mix well, cool.

To prevent pastry from drying out, cover with a damp tea-towel until you are ready to use it.

Layer 2 sheets of pastry together, brushing each with a little extra butter. Cut layered sheets into 4 strips lengthways. Place 1 tablespoon of potato mixture at 1 end of each strip. Fold a corner end of pastry diagonally across filling to other edge to form a triangle. Continue folding to end of strip, retaining triangular shape. Brush triangles with a little more of the extra butter, sprinkle with cumin seeds. Repeat with remaining pastry, filling, extra butter and seeds. Place triangles on lightly greased oven trays. Bake in moderately hot oven about 20 minutes or until lightly browned.

Makes 28.

- Recipe can be prepared a day ahead.
- Storage: Covered, in refrigerator.
- Freeze: Uncooked triangles suitable.
- Microwave: Potatoes suitable.

LAYERED POTATO CAKE

7 large (2kg) potatoes,
  peeled, chopped
60g butter
1 tablespoon milk
¼ cup (20g) grated parmesan cheese
¼ cup (25g) grated mozzarella
  cheese

SALAMI MIXTURE
⅓ cup (45g) drained chopped
  sun-dried tomatoes
50g spicy salami, chopped
1 tablespoon cream

CHEESE MIXTURE
⅓ cup (40g) grated tasty
  cheddar cheese
⅓ cup (25g) grated parmesan cheese
1 tablespoon cream
1 egg yolk

PESTO
1 cup firmly packed fresh basil leaves
2 tablespoons pine nuts, toasted
1 clove garlic
2 tablespoons olive oil
2 tablespoons grated parmesan
  cheese

Grease 22cm springform tin. Boil, steam or microwave potatoes until tender; drain. Mash potatoes with butter and milk until smooth; divide into 3 equal portions.

Stir salami mixture into 1 portion of potato mixture; spread evenly over base of prepared tin. Stir cheese mixture into another portion of potato mixture; spread over salami layer.

Combine pesto with remaining portion of potato mixture; spread over cheese layer. Sprinkle with combined cheeses. Place tin on oven tray, bake, uncovered, in moderately hot oven about 35 minutes or until browned.

Salami Mixture: Combine all ingredients in bowl; mix well.

Cheese Mixture: Combine all ingredients in bowl; mix well.

Pesto: Process basil, nuts and garlic until chopped. While motor is operating, add oil in a thin stream, process until combined. Add cheese; process until combined.

Serves 8.

■ Recipe can be made a day ahead.
■ Storage: Covered, in refrigerator.
■ Freeze: Not suitable.
■ Microwave: Potatoes suitable.

POTATO AND ONION TART

1½ cups (225g) plain flour
125g cold butter, chopped
1 egg yolk
3 teaspoons iced water,
    approximately
1⅓ cups (330ml) olive oil
2 medium (400g) potatoes, peeled,
    thinly sliced
2 medium (300g) onions, sliced
3 eggs, lightly beaten
¼ cup (60ml) cream
ground black pepper

Sift flour into bowl, rub in butter (or process flour and butter until mixture resembles breadcrumbs). Add egg yolk and enough water to make ingredients just cling together (or process until ingredients just come together). Press dough into a ball, knead gently on lightly floured surface until smooth. Wrap in plastic, refrigerate 30 minutes.

Roll pastry between sheets of baking paper until large enough to line 24cm round loose-base flan tin. Lift pastry into tin, ease into side, trim edge. Prick base with fork, refrigerate 30 minutes.

Cover pastry with baking paper, fill with dried beans or rice, place on oven tray. Bake in moderately hot oven 10 minutes. Remove paper and beans carefully from pastry case, bake further 10 minutes or until lightly browned; cool.

Heat oil in large shallow pan, add potatoes in single layer, slightly overlapping, cook, covered, over low heat, turning occasionally, about 10 minutes or until potatoes are tender but not browned. Add onions, cook, covered, until onions are soft; drain, cool.

Whisk eggs, cream and pepper together in a bowl. Carefully pour potato mixture into pastry case, pour egg mixture over potatoes. Bake in moderate oven, 35 minutes or until just set.

Serves 6 to 8.

■ Recipe can be made a day ahead.
■ Storage: Covered, in refrigerator.
■ Freeze: Not suitable.
■ Microwave: Not suitable.

STEAK AND KUMARA PASTIES

300g rump steak
½ small (125g) kumara, peeled
1 small (120g) old potato, peeled
1 small (150g) swede
1 small (80g) onion
1 tablespoon chopped fresh parsley
2 green shallots, chopped
1 egg yolk

PASTRY
3 cups (450g) plain flour
100g butter, chopped
80g lard
½ cup (125ml) water

TOMATO SAUCE
1 cup (250ml) tomato sauce
1 teaspoon Worcestershire sauce

Cut steak and vegetables into 5mm cubes. Combine steak, vegetables, parsley and shallots in bowl. Divide pastry into 2 portions. Roll 1 portion between sheets of baking paper until 3mm thick. Cut pastry into 6 x 12cm rounds; top each round with ¼ cup steak mixture. Lightly brush edges with egg yolk, fold over, pinch edges together to seal. Repeat with remaining pastry, filling and egg yolk.

Place pasties on greased oven trays, brush with remaining egg yolk. Bake in moderate oven about 25 minutes or until browned. Serve with tomato sauce.

Pastry: Sift flour into bowl, rub in butter and lard. Stir in enough water to make ingredients cling together. Press dough into a ball, knead on floured surface until smooth, cover, refrigerate 30 minutes.

Tomato Sauce: Combine ingredients in small bowl.

Makes 12.

■ Pasties can be made 2 days ahead.
■ Storage: Covered, in refrigerator.
■ Freeze: Cooked pasties suitable.
■ Microwave: Not suitable.

LEFT: From back: Potato and Onion Tart, Layered Potato Cake.
RIGHT: Steak and Kumara Pasties.

Left: Wooden platter and china from Corso De' Fiori; tin dish and pepper mill from Accoutrement.
Right: Basket and glasses from Accoutrement.

GNOCCHI WITH TWO SAUCES

**4 large (1.2kg) old potatoes,
    peeled, chopped**
1 egg
1 egg yolk
pinch nutmeg
ground black pepper
**1½ cups (225g) plain flour,
    approximately**
1 tablespoon olive oil

TOMATO SAUCE
1 tablespoon olive oil
1 small (80g) onion, chopped
1 clove garlic, crushed
425g can tomatoes
¼ cup (60ml) dry red wine
1 teaspoon sugar
2 teaspoons chopped fresh thyme

CREAMY BACON AND OLIVE SAUCE
2 bacon rashers, sliced
4 green shallots, chopped
⅓ cup (80ml) dry white wine
300ml cream
¼ cup (20g) grated parmesan cheese
**¼ cup (40g) seedless black
    olives, halved**

Boil, steam or microwave potatoes until tender; drain. Push potatoes through fine sieve into large bowl; cool 10 minutes.

Using 1 hand, work in egg, egg yolk, nutmeg, pepper and enough flour to mix to a soft dough. Knead dough on floured surface until smooth.

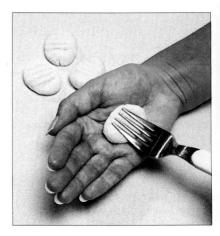

Roll 2 level teaspoons of dough into an oval; place in palm of hand. Using a floured fork, press oval to indent and flatten slightly. Repeat with rest of mixture.

Add gnocchi to large pan of boiling water, simmer, uncovered, about 3 minutes or until gnocchi float to surface and are tender. Drain gnocchi; gently toss through olive oil, serve gnocchi with tomato sauce or creamy bacon and olive sauce.

Tomato Sauce: Heat oil in pan, add onion and garlic, cook, stirring, until onion is soft. Blend or process onion mixture with undrained crushed tomatoes, wine and sugar until smooth. Heat sauce in pan with thyme, simmer, uncovered, a few minutes or until sauce thickens slightly.

Creamy Bacon and Olive Sauce: Cook bacon in dry pan until crisp, add shallots, cook, stirring, until shallots are tender. Add wine, simmer until reduced to 1 tablespoon. Stir in cream, simmer, uncovered, a few minutes or until sauce thickens slightly. Stir in cheese and olives.

Serves 6.

- Sauces can be made a day ahead.
- Storage: Covered, in refrigerator.
- Freeze: Tomato sauce suitable.
- Microwave: Sauces and potatoes suitable.

LEFT: From back: Gnocchi with Creamy Bacon and Olive Sauce, Gnocchi with Tomato Sauce.
BELOW: From left: Green Pea and Potato Soup, Potato Soup with Sausage and Spinach.

Left: China from Waterford Wedgwood.

POTATO SOUP WITH SAUSAGE AND SPINACH

200g chorizo sausage
1 tablespoon olive oil
1 large (200g) red Spanish onion, chopped
2 cloves garlic, crushed
5 medium (1kg) potatoes, peeled
1.5 litres (6 cups) chicken stock
1 bunch (650g) English spinach, shredded

Cut sausage into 5cm strips, cook in dry pan until browned, drain on absorbent paper. Heat oil in pan, add onion and garlic, cook, stirring, until onion is soft. Cut potatoes into 2cm cubes, add potatoes and stock to onion mixture, simmer, uncovered, until potatoes are tender. Add spinach, stir over heat until spinach is wilted. Add sausage, stir until hot.

Serves 6.

- Recipe can be made 2 days ahead.
- Storage: Covered, in refrigerator.
- Freeze: Suitable.
- Microwave: Not suitable.

GREEN PEA AND POTATO SOUP

3 cups (750ml) chicken stock
3 medium (600g) potatoes, peeled, chopped
2 cups (250g) frozen peas
1 tablespoon olive oil
1 small (80g) onion, chopped
1 clove garlic, crushed
2 cups (500ml) water
¼ cup (20g) grated parmesan cheese

Bring stock to boil in pan, add potatoes, boil, uncovered, 5 minutes. Stir in peas, boil further 5 minutes or until potatoes are tender. Heat oil in separate pan, add onion and garlic, cook, stirring, until onion is soft.

Blend or process potato mixture in batches until smooth, return to pan, stir in water and onion mixture, simmer, stirring, until heated through. Serve soup sprinkled with cheese.

Serves 4 to 6.

- Recipe can be made 3 hours ahead.
- Storage: Covered, in refrigerator.
- Freeze: Suitable.
- Microwave: Suitable.

POTATO TERRINE

2 large (600g) old potatoes, peeled
4 medium (800g) red peppers
1 medium (330g) eggplant
½ cup (125ml) light olive oil
1 large (500g) leek
⅓ cup (80ml) light olive oil, extra
3 cloves garlic, crushed
2 tablespoons chopped fresh thyme
1 teaspoon freshly ground
black pepper
10 slices (100g) prosciutto
250g mozzarella cheese, sliced
1 cup lightly packed fresh basil leaves

SAFFRON VINAIGRETTE
½ cup (125ml) light olive oil
2 tablespoons lemon juice
¼ teaspoon saffron powder

Grease 14cm x 21cm loaf pan. Cut potatoes into 2mm slices. Add potatoes to pan of boiling water, cook about 4 minutes or until potatoes are just beginning to soften; drain. Quarter peppers, remove seeds and membranes. Grill peppers, skin side up, until skin blisters and blackens; peel skin away. Cut eggplant lengthways into 5mm slices. Heat half the oil in pan, add half the eggplant, cook until browned on both sides; drain on absorbent paper. Repeat with remaining eggplant and oil. Remove most of the green part from leek, cut white part into 7cm lengths;

cut lengths in half. Boil, steam or microwave leek until tender. Drain leek, rinse under cold water; drain. Combine extra oil, garlic, thyme and pepper in bowl.

Cover base and long sides of prepared pan with prosciutto, allowing prosciutto to overhang edges.

Place half the potatoes, overlapping, over the base, brush with herbed oil mixture; top with half the cheese, brush again with herbed oil. Place all the peppers in a layer, then all the eggplant, all the basil and all the leek, brushing each layer with herbed oil. Top with remaining cheese and then the rest of the potato, brushing with herbed oil between layers; press down firmly. Bring overhanging prosciutto slices to overlap on top of terrine.

Cover top with foil, place terrine on oven tray. Bake in moderate oven 1 hour; uncover, bake further 40 minutes or until filling is tender. Remove from oven, pour off any liquid. Cover top of terrine with plastic wrap, weight with 2 large cans of fruit, for example, for 1 hour. Serve terrine sliced with saffron vinaigrette.

Saffron Vinaigrette: Combine all ingredients in jar; shake well.

Serves 8.

- Recipe can be made a day ahead.
- Storage: Covered, in refrigerator.
- Freeze: Not suitable.
- Microwave: Leek and potatoes suitable.

POTATO SORREL SOUP

40g butter
2 medium (700g) leeks, sliced
4 medium (800g) potatoes,
   peeled, chopped
2 cups (500ml) chicken stock
2 cups (500ml) water
2 bunches (150g) sorrel
½ cup (125ml) cream

Heat butter in pan, add leeks, cook, stir-ring occasionally, about 15 minutes or until leeks are soft. Add potatoes, stock and water, simmer, covered, about 20 minutes or until potatoes are tender. Remove any large stems from sorrel; chop leaves. Add sorrel to potato mixture, cook, stirring, until sorrel is just wilted.

Blend or process mixture in batches until smooth; return to pan, stir in cream, simmer, stirring, until heated through.

Serves 4.

■ Recipe can be made 2 days ahead.
■ Storage: Covered, in refrigerator.
■ Freeze: Suitable.
■ Microwave: Suitable.

POTATO, GARLIC AND CARROT SOUP

2 medium bulbs (140g) garlic
1 tablespoon olive oil
1 medium (150g) onion, chopped
2 medium (400g) old potatoes,
   peeled, chopped
3 large (540g) carrots,
   peeled, chopped
1.5 litres (6 cups) chicken stock
1 tablespoon finely chopped
   fresh thyme
½ cup (125ml) cream

Place whole unpeeled garlic on oven tray, bake, uncovered, in moderately hot oven about 50 minutes or until garlic is soft.

Cool garlic 10 minutes; cut in half, carefully squeeze out garlic.

Heat oil in pan, add onion, cook, stirring, until onion is soft. Add garlic, potatoes, carrots and stock, simmer, uncovered, about 20 minutes or until vegetables are tender. Blend or process mixture in batches until smooth, return to pan; add thyme and cream, simmer, stirring, until heated through.

Serves 6 to 8.

■ Recipe can be made 3 days ahead.
■ Storage: Covered, in refrigerator.
■ Freeze: Suitable.
■ Microwave: Not suitable.

LEFT: Potato Terrine.
ABOVE: From back: Potato, Garlic and Carrot Soup, Potato Sorrel Soup.

Left: China and glassware from Country Road Homewear. Above: China from Waterford Wedgwood.

POTATO CAKES WITH OLIVE PASTE AND RED PEPPER

1 large (300g) red pepper
2 large (600g) old potatoes, peeled
1 small (80g) onion, grated
1/2 cup (75g) self-raising flour
2 eggs, lightly beaten
1/3 cup (80ml) olive oil
180g smoked cheese
2 tablespoons bottled black olive paste

Quarter pepper, remove seeds and membranes. Grill pepper, skin side up, until skin blisters and blackens. Cool about 10 minutes; peel away skin, cut pepper into strips.

Coarsely grate potatoes, press between layers of absorbent paper to remove as much moisture as possible.

Combine potatoes, onion, flour and eggs in bowl; mix well. Divide mixture into 8 portions, shape into 8cm cakes.

Heat oil in heavy-based pan, add cakes in batches, cook until browned on both sides. Place cakes on oven tray, bake in moderate oven about 20 minutes or until cooked through. Serve cakes with sliced cheese, olive paste and strips of roasted red pepper.

Serves 4.

- Potato cakes can be made a day ahead. Reheat in moderate oven just before serving. Peppers can be made 3 days ahead.
- Storage: Covered, separately, in refrigerator.
- Freeze: Not suitable.
- Microwave: Not suitable.

BACON AND CHIVE POTATO PATTIES

3 bacon rashers
2 large (600g) old potatoes, peeled
1/4 cup chopped fresh chives
1/2 cup (125ml) sour cream
1/3 cup (80ml) olive oil

Remove bacon fat from bacon, chop bacon finely. Coarsely grate potatoes, press between layers of absorbent paper to remove as much moisture as possible.

Combine bacon, potatoes, chives and sour cream in bowl; mix well. Divide mixture into 8 portions, shape into 8cm patties. Heat oil in heavy-based pan, add patties in batches, cook until browned on both sides. Place patties in a single layer on oven tray, bake, uncovered, in moderate oven about 20 minutes or until cooked through.

Makes 8.

- Recipe best made just before serving.
- Storage: Covered, in refrigerator.
- Freeze: Not suitable.
- Microwave: Not suitable.

POTATO PANCAKES WITH WARM HERB TOMATOES

1 medium (200g) old potato, peeled, chopped
1 cup (150g) self-raising flour
pinch bicarbonate of soda
1 egg, lightly beaten
3/4 cup (180ml) milk
2 teaspoons chopped fresh oregano
1 teaspoon seasoned pepper
30g butter

WARM HERB TOMATOES
250g cherry tomatoes, quartered
2 tablespoons olive oil
1 tablespoon chopped fresh oregano
1/2 cup (60g) seedless black olives, chopped
1 clove garlic, crushed
4 green shallots, chopped

Boil, steam or microwave potato until tender; mash well. Sift flour and soda into bowl, make well in centre, stir in potato, egg, milk, oregano and pepper. Heat butter in large pan, drop 2 tablespoons of mixture into pan, cook until browned on both sides; repeat with remaining mixture. Serve with warm herb tomatoes.

Warm Herb Tomatoes: Combine all ingredients in small baking dish, bake, uncovered, in moderately hot oven 15 minutes or until ingredients are heated through.

Serves 4.

- Recipe best made close to serving.
- Freeze: Pancakes suitable.
- Microwave: Potato suitable.

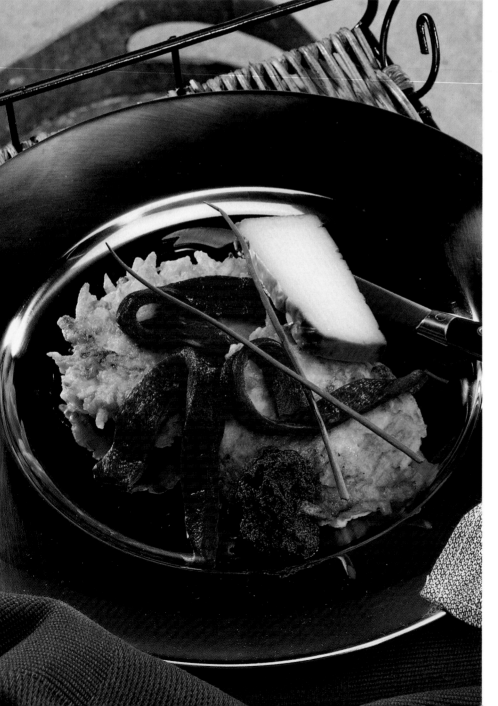

LEFT: Potato Cakes with Olive Paste and Red Pepper.
RIGHT: From back: Potato Pancakes with Warm Herb Tomatoes, Bacon and Chive Potato Patties.

Right: China from Accoutrement.

SOUFFLED POTATOES

**2 large (600g) old
 potatoes, peeled
4 cloves garlic, peeled
2 tablespoons olive oil
½ cup (125ml) thickened cream
¼ cup (35g) drained chopped
 sun-dried tomatoes
2 teaspoons chopped fresh thyme
2 eggs, separated
2 egg whites**

Grease 4 souffle dishes (¾ cup/180ml capacity). Chop potatoes into 4cm pieces. Place potatoes and garlic in small baking dish, drizzle with oil, bake, covered, in moderate oven about 1½ hours or until potatoes and garlic are very soft.

Push undrained potato and garlic mixture through fine sieve into a large bowl. Mixture will look grainy at this stage. Stir in cream, tomatoes, thyme and egg yolks. Beat the 4 egg whites in small bowl with electric mixer until soft peaks form, stir half the egg whites into potato mixture. Gently fold in remaining egg whites. Spoon potato mixture evenly into prepared dishes; place on oven tray. Bake souffles in moderately hot oven about 25 minutes or until lightly browned and puffed.

Serves 4.

- Recipe must be made just before serving.
- Freeze: Not suitable.
- Microwave: Not suitable.

BELOW: Souffled Potatoes.

Below: Souffle dishes and marble from The Bay Tree Kitchen Shop.

BAKED ANCHOVY AND BLUE CHEESE POTATOES

**4 large (1.2kg) old potatoes
1 small (60g) bulb garlic
1 small (150g) red pepper
56g can anchovy fillets,
 drained, chopped
1 small (100g) tomato, peeled, seeded
1 tablespoon sour cream
2 teaspoons chopped fresh oregano
60g blue vein cheese**

Wash, scrub and dry potatoes. Place potatoes and whole garlic bulb on oven tray. Bake in moderately hot oven about 1 hour or until potatoes are tender.

Quarter pepper, remove seeds and membranes. Grill pepper, skin side up, until skin blisters and blackens. Peel away skin, finely chop pepper. Cut top off potatoes, carefully scoop out flesh, leaving skin intact, place flesh in bowl. Cut garlic in half, squeeze garlic into bowl with potato flesh, stir in pepper, anchovies, finely chopped tomato, cream and oregano. Spoon potato mixture back into potato shells; place on oven tray.

Cut cheese into 4 pieces, place a piece on each potato. Bake in moderately hot oven about 10 minutes or until cheese is melted and potatoes heated through.

Serves 4.

- Recipe can be made 3 hours ahead.
- Storage: Covered, in refrigerator.
- Freeze: Not suitable.
- Microwave: Potatoes suitable.

DAUPHINE POTATOES

2 large (600g) potatoes, peeled, chopped
½ cup (125ml) water
30g butter, chopped
½ cup (75g) plain flour
3 eggs
vegetable oil for deep-frying

Boil, steam or microwave potatoes until tender; drain, push through sieve, cool.

Combine water and butter in small pan, bring to boil, stirring, until butter is melted. Add sifted flour all at once, stir vigorously over heat until mixture leaves side of pan and forms a smooth ball. Transfer mixture to small bowl of electric mixer, add eggs 1 at a time, beating well after each addition. Add mashed potato in 2 batches, beat until well combined.

Spoon potato mixture into piping bag fitted with 1cm fluted tube. Heat oil in large pan, pipe 5cm lengths of potato mixture into hot oil, cutting with scissors, deep-fry until golden brown. Drain on absorbent paper. Serve hot, sprinkled with salt, if desired.

Makes about 60.

- ■ Recipe must be made just before serving.
- ■ Freeze: Not suitable.
- ■ Microwave: Potatoes suitable.

LEFT: From left: Potato Quesadilla with Guacamole, Baked Anchovy and Blue Cheese Potato.
BELOW: Dauphine Potatoes.

Left: China and basket from Corso De' Fiori; tiles from Country Floors. Below: Glassware and tea-towel from Accoutrement.

POTATO QUESADILLA WITH GUACAMOLE

1 large (300g) potato,
   peeled, quartered
100g chorizo sausage, chopped
2 large (500g) tomatoes,
   peeled, chopped
3 green shallots, chopped
6 x 16cm round tortillas
1 cup (125g) grated tasty
   cheddar cheese
1 egg white, lightly beaten
1 tablespoon light olive oil

GUACAMOLE
1 large (320g) avocado
½ cup (125ml) sour cream
1 tablespoon lemon juice
1 tablespoon mild sweet chilli sauce

Boil, steam or microwave potato until tender; drain, slice. Combine sausage, tomatoes and shallots in pan, cook, stirring, about 5 minutes or until slightly thickened. Stir in potato.

Dip each tortilla quickly into large bowl of very hot water, place on tea-towel. Divide potato filling between tortillas, top with cheese, brush edges with egg white, fold over to enclose filling; press firmly to seal. Place on greased oven trays, brush with oil, bake in moderately hot oven about 20 minutes or until browned and puffed. Serve with guacamole.

Guacamole: Blend or process all ingredients until smooth.

Makes 6.

- ■ Potato filling can be made a day ahead.
- ■ Storage: Covered, in refrigerator.
- ■ Freeze: Not suitable.
- ■ Microwave: Potato suitable.

ASPARAGUS WITH POTATOES AND WILD RICE

You will need to cook ¼ cup (45g) wild rice for this recipe.

2 bunches (500g) fresh asparagus

POTATOES AND WILD RICE
2 medium (400g) old potatoes
1 tablespoon olive oil
20g butter
2 bacon rashers, chopped
1 clove garlic, crushed
¾ cup (180ml) cream
½ cup cooked wild rice
⅓ cup (35g) drained sun-dried tomatoes, chopped
1 tablespoon chopped fresh thyme

Boil, steam or microwave asparagus until tender, serve with potato mixture.

Potatoes and Wild Rice: Peel and cut potatoes into 1cm cubes. Heat oil and butter in pan, add potatoes, bacon and garlic, cook, stirring, until potatoes are tender; drain on absorbent paper.

Return potato mixture to pan, stir in cream, rice, tomatoes and thyme, simmer, uncovered, about 3 minutes or until cream thickens slightly.

Serves 4.

- Potatoes and wild rice can be prepared 3 hours ahead.
- Storage: Covered, in refrigerator.
- Freeze: Not suitable.
- Microwave: Asparagus suitable.

BELOW: Asparagus with Potatoes and Wild Rice.
RIGHT: From left: Potato Cakes with Sweet Peppers, Spanish Omelette.

Below: Basket and tea-towel from Accoutrement.
Right: Plates from Hale Imports, glasses from Morris Home & Garden Wares, ceramic planter from Parker's of Turramurra.

SPANISH OMELETTE

1½ cups (375ml) olive oil
3 medium (600g) potatoes, peeled,
    thinly sliced
1 medium (150g) onion, sliced
6 eggs, lightly beaten

Heat oil in pan, add potatoes, cook,
covered, about 15 minutes, turning occasionally, until tender, but not browned.
Add onion, cook, covered, until soft.
Strain mixture through coarse sieve;
reserve 1 tablespoon oil, cool.

Combine potato mixture and eggs in a
bowl. Heat reserved oil in pan, add potato
mixture, cook 2 minutes or until omelette
is partly set and lightly browned. Carefully
slide omelette onto large plate, invert into
same pan, cook other side about 2 minutes
or until set and lightly browned. Cool 20
minutes before serving.

Serves 4 to 6.

■ Recipe best made 20 minutes
   before serving.
■ Microwave: Not suitable.
■ Freeze: Not suitable.

POTATO CAKES WITH SWEET PEPPERS

3 medium (600g) old potatoes,
    peeled, chopped
2 egg yolks
2 tablespoons chopped fresh
    coriander
4 green shallots, chopped
¼ cup (20g) grated parmesan cheese
¼ cup (30g) grated tasty
    cheddar cheese
½ teaspoon sambal oelek
1 clove garlic, crushed
plain flour
2 tablespoons olive oil

SWEET PEPPERS
1 tablespoon olive oil
1 small (80g) onion, sliced
2 teaspoons sugar
2 medium (400g) red peppers
2 teaspoons balsamic vinegar
1 teaspoon chopped fresh thyme
1 teaspoon chopped fresh oregano

Boil, steam or microwave potatoes until
tender, rinse under cold water; drain,
mash. Combine mashed potato, egg
yolks, coriander, shallots, cheeses, sambal oelek and garlic in bowl; mix well.

Using floured hands, shape mixture
into 8 patties; roll patties in flour, shake
away excess flour. Heat oil in pan, add
patties, cook until browned on both sides.
Serve with sweet peppers.

Sweet Peppers: Heat oil in pan, add
onion and sugar, cook, stirring, until onion
is browned. Quarter peppers, remove
seeds and membranes, grill peppers, skin
side up, until skin blisters and blackens;
peel skin away. Cut peppers into thin
strips. Combine onion, peppers, vinegar
and herbs in bowl; cover, refrigerate.

Serves 4.

■ Sweet peppers can be made
   2 days ahead.
■ Storage: Covered, in refrigerator.
■ Freeze: Not suitable.
■ Microwave: Potatoes suitable.

CREAM OF POTATO SOUP

1 tablespoon olive oil
2 medium (300g) onions, chopped
5 medium (1kg) old potatoes,
    peeled, chopped
1.5 litres (6 cups) chicken stock
300ml cream

Heat oil in pan, add onions, cook, stirring, until soft. Add potatoes and stock, simmer, uncovered, about 20 minutes or until potatoes are tender. Blend or process mixture in batches until smooth, return to pan; add cream, simmer, stirring, until heated through.

Serves 8.
- Recipe can be made a day ahead.
- Storage: Covered, in refrigerator.
- Freeze: Suitable.
- Microwave: Suitable.

SOUP VARIATIONS

OREGANO AND
SUN-DRIED TOMATOES
¼ cup (35g) drained sun-dried
    tomatoes, finely chopped
¼ cup finely chopped fresh oregano

Stir tomatoes and oregano into cream of potato soup before reheating.

PARMESAN CHEESE AND SAGE
½ cup (40g) finely grated parmesan
    cheese
2 tablespoons finely chopped
    fresh sage

Stir cheese and sage into cream of potato soup before reheating.

CORN AND
WORCESTERSHIRE SAUCE
130g can corn kernels, rinsed, drained
130g can creamed corn
2 tablespoons Worcestershire sauce

Stir corn and sauce into cream of potato soup before reheating.

PROSCIUTTO AND SOUR CREAM

150g prosciutto, chopped
300ml sour cream
1½ teaspoons sambal oelek

Cook prosciutto in dry pan over high heat until crisp. Mix cream and sambal oelek in bowl. Serve cream of potato soup topped with sour cream mixture and prosciutto.

SMOKED SALMON AND DILL

150g smoked salmon, finely chopped
1½ tablespoons chopped fresh dill
2 tablespoons lemon juice

Stir salmon, dill and juice into cream of potato soup before reheating.

BAKED POTATO SKINS

5 medium (1kg) old potatoes
2 tablespoons olive oil
2 teaspoons fine sea salt
1 teaspoon seasoned pepper
2 teaspoons chopped fresh rosemary
300ml sour cream

Makes 30.

■ Skins can be prepared a day ahead.
■ Storage: Covered, in refrigerator.
■ Freeze: Not suitable.
■ Microwave: Whole potatoes suitable.

Scrub potatoes well, brush with half the oil, bake in hot oven about 50 minutes or until tender, cool. Cut each potato into 6 wedges, carefully scoop out flesh, leaving skins intact (reserve potato flesh for another use).

Place potato skins in single layer on wire rack over oven tray, skin side up, brush with remaining oil, sprinkle with combined salt, pepper and rosemary.

Just before serving, bake in hot oven about 30 minutes or until crisp. Serve hot with sour cream.

LEFT: Prosciutto and Sour Cream variation of Cream of Potato Soup.
ABOVE: Baked Potato Skins.

Above: Setting from Grace Bros.

19

QUARTET OF CROQUETTES

BASIC POTATO MIXTURE
5 medium (1kg) old potatoes,
 peeled, chopped
2 egg yolks
2 tablespoons cream
plain flour
2 eggs, lightly beaten
1½ cups (150g) packaged
 breadcrumbs
vegetable oil for deep-frying

Boil, steam or microwave potatoes until tender; drain, mash well. Stir in egg yolks and cream; cool. Refrigerate 30 minutes.

Shape ¼ cup of the basic potato mixture into croquette shape, roll in flour, shake away excess flour, dip in eggs, then breadcrumbs. Repeat with remaining potato mixture, flour, eggs and breadcrumbs. Place on oven tray, cover, refrigerate 30 minutes or until firm. Just before serving, deep-fry croquettes in hot oil until golden brown.

Makes 12.

- ■ Recipe can be prepared a day ahead.
- ■ Storage: Covered, in refrigerator.
- ■ Freeze: Suitable.
- ■ Microwave: Potatoes suitable.

CROQUETTE VARIATIONS

SMOKED SALMON
100g smoked salmon, finely chopped
2 tablespoons chopped fresh dill
1 tablespoon lemon juice

Combine all ingredients in bowl with basic potato mixture; mix well.

CHICKEN AND CORN
2 x 130g cans corn kernels,
 rinsed, drained
1½ cups (225g) chopped
 cooked chicken
¼ cup chopped fresh parsley
1½ teaspoons chicken stock powder

Combine all ingredients in bowl with basic potato mixture; mix well.

CURRY AND CORIANDER
40g butter
1 tablespoon vegetable oil
1 medium (150g) onion, chopped
1½ tablespoons mild curry powder
2 teaspoons ground cumin
1 tablespoon lime juice
⅓ cup chopped fresh coriander

Heat butter and oil in pan, add onion, curry powder and cumin, cook, stirring, until onion is soft; cool. Combine onion mixture, juice and coriander in bowl with basic potato mixture; mix well.

CHEESE AND HERB
2 tablespoons chopped fresh parsley
⅓ cup chopped fresh chives
⅔ cup (80g) grated tasty cheddar cheese
⅓ cup (25g) grated parmesan cheese

Combine all ingredients in bowl with basic potato mixture; mix well.

TARAMOSALATA

1 large (300g) old potato,
**   peeled, chopped**
100g tarama
1 tablespoon lemon juice
¼ cup (60ml) white vinegar
½ small (40g) onion, finely grated
1 cup (250ml) extra light olive oil

Boil, steam or microwave potato until tender; cool, refrigerate until cold. Blend or process potato, tarama, juice, vinegar, onion and oil until smooth.

Serves 6.

- Recipe can be made 3 days ahead.
- Storage: Covered, in refrigerator.
- Freeze: Not suitable.
- Microwave: Potato suitable.

GREEK POTATO GARLIC DIP

1 medium (70g) bulb garlic
2 medium (400g) old potatoes,
**   peeled, quartered**
½ cup (125ml) extra virgin olive oil
½ cup (125ml) vegetable oil
2 tablespoons white wine vinegar
1 teaspoon chopped fresh thyme
¼ cup (60ml) chicken stock

Place whole garlic bulb on oven tray, bake, uncovered, in moderately hot oven 50 minutes. Cool 10 minutes, cut in half, carefully squeeze out garlic.

Boil, steam or microwave potatoes until tender; drain. Beat garlic and warm potatoes in medium bowl with electric mixer until combined. Add oils gradually in a thin stream while motor is operating, then add vinegar and thyme, beat until smooth; stir in stock. Serve with prawns or vegetable crudites, if desired.

Serves 6.

- Dip can be made a day ahead but will thicken slightly.
- Storage: Covered, in refrigerator.
- Freeze: Not suitable.
- Microwave: Potatoes suitable.

LEFT: Chicken and Corn variation of Quartet of Croquettes.
BELOW: From back: Greek Potato Garlic Dip, Taramosalata.

Left: Plate from The Bay Tree Kitchen Shop; serviette from Accoutrement; glasses from Home & Garden on the Mall. Below: Plate from Country Road Homewear; tray and bowl from Accoutrement.

POTATO AND KUMARA CRISPS
5 medium (1kg) old potatoes
2 medium (800g) kumara
vegetable oil for deep-frying

CHERRY TOMATO SAUCE
250g cherry tomatoes
1 clove garlic, crushed
1 tablespoon lemon juice
1 tablespoon mild sweet chilli sauce
¼ teaspoon ground black pepper
½ cup (125ml) light olive oil

Peel potatoes and kumara, cut into 1mm slices, placing slices into a bowl of cold water. Drain potato slices, pat dry. Deep-fry potato slices in hot oil in batches, turning occasionally, until lightly browned. Drain in single layers on absorbent paper. Serve with cherry tomato sauce.
Cherry Tomato Sauce: Blend or process all ingredients until smooth.

Serves 8.

- ■ Recipe can be made a day ahead.
- ■ Storage: Cold crisps, in airtight container. Sauce, covered, in refrigerator.
- ■ Freeze: Not suitable.
- ■ Microwave: Not suitable.

FRIED NEW POTATOES WITH CHILLI MARMALADE

30 baby (1.2kg) new potatoes
vegetable oil for deep-frying
⅔ cup (160ml) sour cream
30 fresh coriander leaves

CHILLI MARMALADE
2 tablespoons olive oil
1 medium (150g) onion,
finely chopped
1 medium (200g) red pepper,
thinly sliced
1 clove garlic, crushed
3 teaspoons mild sweet chilli sauce
2 teaspoons caster sugar
1 teaspoon white wine vinegar

Boil, steam or microwave potatoes until just tender; drain, cool (do not rinse). Using a melon baller, scoop a small hollow in each potato; discard scooped-out pieces. Deep-fry potatoes in hot oil in batches until golden brown; drain on absorbent paper.

Using a piping bag fitted with small plain tube, pipe sour cream into potato hollows, top with a little chilli marmalade and a coriander leaf.

Chilli Marmalade: Heat oil in small pan, add onion, pepper, garlic and sauce, cook, stirring occasionally, over low heat, about 10 minutes or until vegetables are very soft. Add sugar and vinegar, cook, stirring, about 5 minutes or until almost all the liquid has evaporated. Process until finely chopped.

Makes 30.

■ Recipe best made close to serving.
■ Freeze: Not suitable.
■ Microwave: Potatoes suitable.

SMOKED FISH FRITTERS WITH TOMATO CHILLI SAUCE

2 medium (400g) potatoes,
peeled, chopped
200g smoked fish
1 tablespoon chopped fresh parsley
½ small (40g) onion, finely chopped
2 eggs, lightly beaten
¼ cup (35g) plain flour
vegetable oil for deep-frying

TOMATO CHILLI SAUCE
2 medium (260g) tomatoes,
peeled, seeded
40g butter
1 medium (150g) onion,
finely chopped
2 small fresh red chillies, seeded,
finely chopped
2 cloves garlic, crushed
1 tablespoon chopped fresh parsley

Boil, steam or microwave potatoes until tender. Poach, steam or microwave fish until cooked through; chop fish roughly. Blend or process potatoes, fish, parsley and onion until smooth. Transfer mixture to medium bowl of electric mixer, add eggs and flour, beat until well combined.

Deep-fry tablespoons of mixture in batches in hot oil, turning occasionally, 3 minutes or until browned. Drain on absorbent paper. Serve with tomato chilli sauce.

Tomato Chilli Sauce: Finely chop tomatoes. Melt butter in pan, add onion, chillies and garlic, cook, stirring, until onion is soft. Stir in tomatoes, simmer, uncovered, 10 minutes or until sauce is slightly thickened; stir in parsley.

Serves 6.

■ Fritters best made just before serving. Sauce can be made a day ahead.
■ Storage: Covered, in refrigerator.
■ Freeze: Not suitable.
■ Microwave: Potatoes and fish suitable.

LEFT: Fried New Potatoes with Chilli Marmalade.
ABOVE LEFT: Potato and Kumara Crisps.
ABOVE: Smoked Fish Fritters with Tomato Chilli Sauce.

Left: Platter from Ventura Design; cloth from Morris Home & Garden Wares.

CRAB AND LEMON GRASS DOUBLE CRISPS

3 medium (600g) potatoes
2 tablespoons vegetable oil
170g can crab meat, drained
2 green shallots, chopped
1 teaspoon chopped fresh coriander
1 tablespoon chopped fresh
    lemon grass
1 teaspoon fish sauce
1 tablespoon finely chopped canned
    drained water chestnuts
2 tablespoons plain flour
2 teaspoons water, approximately
vegetable oil for deep-frying

TOMATO GINGER SAUCE
1 tablespoon vegetable oil
4 large (1kg) tomatoes, chopped
1 small (80g) onion, chopped
2 teaspoons grated fresh ginger

Cut potatoes into 1mm slices; you need 48 slices. Brush 2 oven trays with half the oil, place potatoes in single layer on trays, brush with remaining oil. Bake, un-covered, in moderate oven about 10 minutes or until soft but not brown.

POTATO TAMALES

4 medium (800g) old potatoes, peeled
2 cups (500ml) chicken stock
2 tablespoons vegetable oil
1 medium (150g) onion, chopped
1 clove garlic, crushed
1 medium (200g) red pepper,
    finely chopped
1 small fresh red chilli, seeded,
    finely chopped
3 medium (390g) tomatoes, peeled,
    seeded, chopped
1 tablespoon chopped fresh thyme
1 cup (70g) stale breadcrumbs
1 egg, lightly beaten
3 large (1.2kg) corn cobs with husks

Cut potatoes into 2cm cubes. Combine potatoes and stock in pan, simmer, covered, until potatoes are tender. Drain potatoes, mash well, cool 10 minutes. Heat oil in pan, add onion, garlic, pepper and chilli, cook, stirring, until onion is soft. Add tomatoes and thyme, cook, stirring, until tomatoes are soft. Stir in mashed potato, breadcrumbs and egg; cover, refrigerate 1 hour.

Remove husks carefully from corn. You will need 24 husks for this recipe. Reserve corn for another recipe. Divide potato mix-ture into 12 equal portions. Place 1 portion of mixture onto 1 corn husk to form a 6cm square. Fold husk around filling, wrap another husk around to form a parcel, tie with string. Repeat with remaining potato mixture and husks. Place tamales in large steamer over simmering water, cover, steam about 45 minutes or until firm.

Makes 12.

■ Filling can be made a day ahead.
■ Storage: Covered, in refrigerator.
■ Freeze: Not suitable.
■ Microwave: Potatoes suitable.

CURRIED PARSNIP AND POTATO SOUP

50g butter
1 small (200g) leek, chopped
2 small (120g) parsnips, chopped
2 medium (240g) carrots, chopped
2 bacon rashers, chopped
2 teaspoons mild curry powder
3 medium (600g) potatoes,
    peeled, chopped
2 bay leaves
¼ teaspoon ground turmeric
1.25 litres (5 cups) chicken stock
1 tablespoon chopped fresh parsley

Heat butter in pan, add leek, parsnips, carrots and bacon, cook, stirring, about 10 minutes or until leek is soft. Add curry powder, cook, stirring, until fragrant. Add potatoes, bay leaves, turmeric and stock, simmer, covered, until potatoes are tender; discard bay leaves.

Blend or process mixture in batches until smooth; return to pan, simmer, stir-ring, until heated through. Serve soup sprinkled with parsley.

Serves 4 to 6.

■ Soup can be made 3 days ahead.
■ Storage: Covered, in refrigerator.
■ Freeze: Suitable.
■ Microwave: Suitable.

ABOVE: Potato Tamales.
RIGHT: Crab and Lemon Grass Double Crisps.
FAR RIGHT: Curried Parsnip and Potato Soup.

Right: China from Accoutrement. Far right: China from Waterford Wedgwood.

Press excess liquid from crab meat. Combine crab, shallots, coriander, lemon grass, sauce and chestnuts in bowl.

Blend flour with enough of the water to make a thick paste. Brush edge of each potato slice with a little flour paste, place 1 level teaspoon of crab mixture in centre of potato, top with another potato slice; press edges together to seal. Repeat with remaining potato, paste and filling.

Deep-fry double crisps in hot oil in batches until golden brown; drain on absorbent paper. Serve double crisps with tomato ginger sauce.

Tomato Ginger Sauce: Combine oil, tomatoes, onion and ginger in pan, cook, stirring occasionally, about 20 minutes or until onions are very soft. Blend or process mixture until smooth. Push through fine sieve; discard pulp.

Serves 4.

- ■ Recipe best made close to serving.
- ■ Freeze: Not suitable.
- ■ Microwave: Tomato ginger sauce suitable.

KUMARA GINGER FRITTERS

1 tablespoon vegetable oil
1 small (80g) onion, chopped
1 medium (120g) zucchini, grated
2 teaspoons grated fresh ginger
1½ teaspoons mild sweet chilli sauce
1 medium (400g) kumara,
    peeled, grated
1 tablespoon chopped fresh
    coriander
2 eggs, lightly beaten
⅓ cup (50g) plain flour
2 tablespoons sesame seeds
vegetable oil for deep-frying

CHILLI CORIANDER YOGURT
½ cup (125ml) plain yogurt
1 tablespoon chopped fresh
    coriander
2 teaspoons mild sweet chilli sauce

Heat oil in pan, add onion, zucchini, ginger and sauce, cook, stirring, until onion is soft. Transfer onion mixture to a large bowl, stir in kumara, coriander, eggs, flour and seeds.

Just before serving, deep-fry tablespoons of mixture in hot oil until browned and cooked through; drain on absorbent paper. Serve warm fritters with chilli coriander yogurt.

Chilli Coriander Yogurt: Combine all ingredients in bowl.

Makes about 20.

- Chilli coriander yogurt can be made 3 days ahead.
- Storage: Covered, in refrigerator.
- Freeze: Not suitable.
- Microwave: Not suitable.

KUMARA TEMPURA WITH DIPPING SAUCE

2 medium (800g) kumara, peeled
plain flour
vegetable oil for deep-frying

BATTER
1½ cups (225g) plain flour
½ teaspoon baking powder
½ teaspoon salt
1 egg
1 egg yolk
1¾ cups (430ml) water

DIPPING SAUCE
2 tablespoons soy sauce
1 tablespoon mild sweet chilli sauce
¼ teaspoon sesame oil
2 tablespoons water
1 clove garlic, sliced
1 green shallot, sliced

POTATO ROSEMARY CRISPS

**1 medium (200g) old potato,
   peeled, chopped
60g soft butter
1 tablespoon icing sugar mixture
1 egg white
2 tablespoons plain flour
1 tablespoon chopped fresh rosemary
2 teaspoons sesame seeds
1 teaspoon coarse sea salt**

Boil, steam or microwave potato until tender. Mash potato well; cool. You need ½ cup cold mashed potato for this recipe.

Beat butter and sifted icing sugar in small bowl with electric mixer until light and fluffy, add potato and egg white, beat on low speed until just combined. Push mixture through a fine strainer into bowl, stir in sifted flour; mix well. Drop level teaspoons of mixture onto lightly greased oven trays, about 5cm apart.

Using a spatula, spread mixture to 7cm rounds, sprinkle with rosemary, seeds and salt. Bake in moderately hot oven about 7 minutes or until edges are golden brown. Stand about 2 minutes before removing from trays with spatula. Repeat with remaining mixture.

Makes about 36.

■ Recipe can be made 2 days ahead.
■ Storage: Airtight container.
■ Freeze: Not suitable.
■ Microwave: Potato suitable.

LEFT: From left: Kumara Ginger Fritters, Kumara Tempura with Dipping Sauce. BELOW: Potato Rosemary Crisps.

Left: China from Corso De' Fiori; wicker basket from Accoutrement. Below: Plate and cloth from Accoutrement.

Cut kumara into 5mm slices. Boil, steam or microwave kumara until just tender; drain on absorbent paper. Toss kumara slices in flour; shake away excess flour.

Just before serving, dip kumara in batter, deep-fry in hot oil in batches until lightly browned; drain on absorbent paper.
Batter: Sift dry ingredients into bowl, whisk in combined egg, egg yolk and water, whisk until smooth.
Dipping Sauce: Combine all ingredients in bowl; mix well.

Serves 4 to 6.

■ Recipe best made just before serving. Dipping sauce can be made a day ahead.
■ Storage: Covered, in refrigerator.
■ Freeze: Not suitable.
■ Microwave: Kumara suitable.

WELL-DRESSED BAKED POTATOES

4 large (1.2kg) old potatoes

Scrub potatoes well. Pierce skin in several places with fork or skewer. Place potatoes onto oven shelves. Bake in moderately hot oven about 1 hour or until tender. Serve with topping of your choice.

ASPARAGUS AND CHEESE SAUCE

1 bunch (250g) fresh asparagus
40g butter
2 tablespoons plain flour
1½ cups (375ml) milk
1 cup (125g) grated tasty cheddar cheese
¼ cup (20g) flaked almonds, toasted

Cut asparagus into 4cm lengths; boil, steam or microwave until tender. Heat butter in pan, stir in flour, stir over heat until mixture is bubbly. Remove from heat, gradually stir in milk, stir over heat until mixture boils and thickens. Remove from heat, stir in cheese. Divide asparagus between potatoes, top with cheese sauce and sprinkle with nuts.

HOLLANDAISE SAUCE WITH POACHED EGGS

¼ cup (60ml) white vinegar
6 black peppercorns
1 bay leaf
125g butter
2 egg yolks
few drops lemon juice
1 teaspoon chopped drained capers
1 tablespoon French mustard
4 eggs, poached

Combine vinegar, peppercorns and bay leaf in pan, simmer, uncovered, until liquid is reduced by half, strain; reserve liquid.

Beat butter in small bowl of electric mixer until creamy. Whisk egg yolks with a little of the butter in heatproof bowl over pan of simmering water; stir in reserved liquid. Stir until mixture just begins to thicken. Whisk in remaining butter in teaspoonfuls, whisking constantly until all the butter has been added; whisk in lemon juice, capers and mustard. Place an egg on each potato; top with hollandaise sauce.

AVOCADO AND BACON TOPPING

1 teaspoon olive oil
3 bacon rashers, chopped
½ medium (100g) red pepper
1 medium (250g) avocado
1 clove garlic, crushed
¼ cup (60ml) sour cream
1 teaspoon lemon juice
2 drops Tabasco sauce

Heat oil in pan, add bacon, cook, stirring, until crisp; drain on absorbent paper. Cut pepper into thin strips. Place avocado in bowl, mash roughly with a fork. Stir in garlic, cream, juice and sauce. Divide avocado mixture between potatoes, top with bacon and pepper.

SMOKED SALMON AND DILL CREAM TOPPING

½ cup (125ml) sour cream
1 teaspoon chopped fresh dill
1 teaspoon lemon juice
½ teaspoon sugar
200g smoked salmon slices

Combine cream, dill, juice and sugar in bowl; mix well. Divide salmon between potatoes, top with cream mixture.

CARAMELISED ONION AND CHICKEN TOPPING

50g butter
3 medium (450g) onions, sliced
2 tablespoons caster sugar
1 cup (150g) chopped cooked chicken

Heat butter in pan, add onions and sugar. Cook over low heat, stirring occasionally, about 20 minutes or until onions are soft and browned. Divide chicken between potatoes, top with onions.

GARLIC CHEESE AND CHORIZO SAUSAGE TOPPING

250g chorizo sausage, sliced
425g can tomatoes, drained, chopped
1 tablespoon brown sugar
1 teaspoon cider vinegar
80g packet garlic and herb cheese spread

Cook sausage in dry pan about 3 minutes or until heated through; drain on absorbent paper. Combine tomatoes, sugar and vinegar in small bowl; mix well. Divide sausage and cheese spread between potatoes, top with tomato mixture.

BOLOGNESE TOPPING

1 tablespoon olive oil
1 medium (150g) onion, chopped
1 clove garlic, crushed
350g minced beef
425g can tomatoes
2 tablespoons tomato paste
1 teaspoon chopped fresh basil
1 teaspoon chopped fresh oregano
½ cup (100g) canned red kidney beans, rinsed, drained
½ cup (50g) grated mozzarella cheese

Heat oil in pan, add onion and garlic, cook, stirring, until onion is soft. Add mince, cook, stirring, over high heat until mince is browned. Add undrained crushed tomatoes, paste and herbs, simmer, covered, about 20 minutes or until mince is tender and mixture thickens slightly. Add beans, cook, stirring, until hot. Divide between potatoes, top with cheese.

ONION, SOUR CREAM AND GARLIC TOPPING

1 small (80g) onion, grated
2 cloves garlic, crushed
½ cup (125ml) sour cream
½ cup (60g) grated tasty cheddar cheese
2 tablespoons chopped fresh chives

Cut tops off potatoes, carefully scoop out most of the flesh with a spoon, leaving skin intact. Combine hot potato with ingredients in bowl. Spoon mixture back into potato shells.

Each recipe serves 4.

■ Recipes best made just before serving.
■ Freeze: Not suitable.
■ Microwave: Potatoes suitable.

TOP ROW: From left: Asparagus and Cheese Sauce, Avocado and Bacon Topping, Caramelised Onion and Chicken Topping, Bolognese Topping.
BOTTOM ROW: From left: Hollandaise Sauce with Poached Egg, Smoked Salmon and Dill Cream Topping, Garlic Cheese and Chorizo Sausage Topping, Onion, Sour Cream and Garlic Topping.

Main Courses

We've spiced them, buttered them, cooked them crunchy or kept them tender — and that's only a start to the delicious ideas we've had about potatoes for any meal, whether you want something hot and hearty or light and equally tempting. Together, they peel away any ideas that potatoes are dull!

POTATO ALMOND RAVIOLI WITH PUMPKIN SAUCE

2 medium (400g) old potatoes, peeled, chopped
1 egg, lightly beaten
2 cloves garlic, crushed
2 teaspoons chopped fresh oregano
¼ cup (35g) flaked almonds
2 cups (300g) plain flour
3 eggs, lightly beaten, extra
2 tablespoons chopped fresh chives

PUMPKIN SAUCE
500g pumpkin
¾ cup (180ml) chicken stock
¼ cup (60ml) cream
2 teaspoons lemon juice
pinch ground nutmeg

Boil, steam or microwave potatoes until tender; drain, mash. Place potatoes, egg, garlic, oregano and nuts in bowl; mix well.

Sift flour into another bowl, make well in centre, add extra eggs and chives. Using fingers, gradually mix flour into eggs. Press mixture into a ball (or combine flour, extra eggs and chives in food processor, process until mixture forms a ball). Knead dough well for about 10 minutes or until smooth and elastic. Cover dough, stand 20 minutes.

Cut dough in half. Roll each half on lightly floured surface into a rectangular shape, 2mm thick. Place level teaspoons of potato mixture 3cm apart over 1 sheet of pasta. Lightly brush remaining pasta sheet with water, place over filling; press firmly between filling.

Using a pasta wheel, trim neatly around edges of pasta. Cut evenly between filling. Lightly sprinkle ravioli with a little flour.

Just before serving, add ravioli to large pan of boiling water, boil, uncovered, about 3 minutes or until just tender; drain. Serve ravioli with pumpkin sauce.

Pumpkin Sauce: Remove seeds from pumpkin, place piece of pumpkin on oven tray, bake, uncovered, in hot oven about 40 minutes or until tender; cool. Remove skin; mash pumpkin. Combine pumpkin and remaining ingredients in pan, cook, stirring, until heated through. Blend or process mixture until smooth.

Serves 4.

- Recipe can be prepared several hours ahead.
- Storage: Covered, separately, in refrigerator.
- Freeze: Covered, separately.
- Microwave: Potatoes and sauce suitable.

RIGHT: Potato Almond Ravioli with Pumpkin Sauce.

CHICKEN AND NOODLES WITH RED CURRY PASTE

1 large (500g) kumara, peeled
1 tablespoon vegetable oil
750g chicken thigh fillets, sliced
1 cup (250ml) chicken stock
½ cup (125ml) coconut milk
2 teaspoons fish sauce
2 tablespoons chopped fresh
   coriander
⅔ cup (100g) roasted unsalted
   cashews
375g packet fresh egg noodles

RED CURRY PASTE
2 small fresh red chillies
1 tablespoon chopped coriander root
2 cloves garlic, chopped
1 teaspoon ground cumin
2 teaspoons paprika
½ medium (85g) red Spanish onion,
   chopped
¼ cup (60ml) lime juice

Cut kumara into 2cm pieces. Heat oil in pan, add chicken in batches, cook until browned. Combine chicken, kumara and red curry paste in pan, cook, stirring, until fragrant. Stir in stock, simmer, covered, about 10 minutes or until kumara is tender. Stir in coconut milk, sauce, coriander and cashews, stir over heat until heated through.

Add noodles to large pan of boiling water, boil, uncovered, until tender; rinse under hot water, drain. Serve chicken mixture over noodles.

Red Curry Paste: Process all ingredients until smooth.

Serves 4.

- Paste can be made 3 days ahead.
- Storage: Covered, in refrigerator.
- Freeze: Not suitable.
- Microwave: Noodles suitable.

INDIAN-STYLE SPICED CHICKEN

8 (1.6kg) chicken thigh cutlets
1 tablespoon vegetable oil
2 medium (300g) onions, chopped
2 small fresh red chillies, chopped
1 teaspoon ground cinnamon
2 teaspoons cumin seeds
1 tablespoon grated fresh ginger
2 cloves garlic, crushed
2 large (600g) old potatoes,
   peeled, chopped
½ cup (125ml) water
3 medium (390g) tomatoes, peeled,
   seeded, chopped

Remove skin from chicken. Heat oil in pan, add chicken in batches, cook until well browned all over. Remove chicken from pan; drain on absorbent paper.

Drain all but 1 tablespoon of juices from pan, add onions, chillies, cinnamon, seeds, ginger and garlic to pan, cook, stirring, until onions are soft.

Return chicken to pan. Add potatoes, water and tomatoes, simmer, covered, about 15 minutes or until chicken and potatoes are tender.

Serves 4.

- Recipe can be prepared several hours ahead.
- Storage: Covered, in refrigerator.
- Freeze: Not suitable.
- Microwave: Suitable.

CHICKEN AND KUMARA RISOTTO

1 medium (400g) kumara, peeled
2 tablespoons olive oil
1 medium (350g) leek, sliced
500g chicken thigh fillets, sliced
2 cloves garlic, crushed
¼ teaspoon chilli powder
½ teaspoon ground turmeric
1½ cups (300g) short-grain rice
425g can tomatoes
½ cup (125ml) dry white wine
2½ cups (625ml) chicken stock
½ cup (40g) grated parmesan cheese
2 tablespoons chopped fresh basil

Cut kumara into 2cm pieces; boil, steam or microwave kumara until tender. Heat oil in large pan, add leek, chicken, garlic and spices, cook, stirring, 5 minutes. Stir in rice; mix well. Stir in undrained crushed tomatoes and wine, simmer, uncovered, stirring constantly, 10 minutes.

Stir in stock, simmer, covered, 15 minutes, stirring halfway through cooking time. Remove from heat; stand, covered, 10 minutes. Stir in cheese, basil and kumara, stir over heat until hot.

Serves 4.

- Recipe best made just before serving.
- Freeze: Not suitable.
- Microwave: Kumara suitable.

LEFT: Clockwise from left: Indian-Style Spiced Chicken, Chicken and Kumara Risotto, Chicken and Noodles with Red Curry Paste.

Pottery bowls from Kenwick Galleries.

DOUBLE POTATO AND CHICKEN CHEESECAKE

You will need to cook 2 medium (400g) potatoes for this recipe.

200g packet lightly salted potato crisps, finely crushed
40g butter, melted
1 tablespoon chopped fresh parsley
2 tablespoons grated romano cheese

FILLING
1 cup cold mashed potato
⅓ cup (80ml) sour cream
250g packet cream cheese, chopped
3 eggs
⅔ cup (100g) chopped cooked chicken
8 seedless black olives, sliced
½ cup (40g) grated romano cheese
3 green shallots, chopped
¼ cup (35g) drained chopped sun-dried tomatoes

Grease 20cm springform tin, cover base with baking paper. Combine crisps, butter, parsley and cheese in bowl; mix well. Press mixture evenly over base of prepared tin, top with filling; smooth top.

Bake in moderate oven about 1 hour or until cheesecake is browned and firm. Stand 10 minutes before removing from tin; serve warm or cold.

Filling: Beat potato, cream, cream cheese and eggs in medium bowl with electric mixer until smooth. Stir in remaining ingredients.

Serves 6 to 8.

■ Recipe can be made a day ahead.
■ Storage: Covered, in refrigerator.
■ Freeze: Not suitable.
■ Microwave: Not suitable.

CREAMY SHITAKE QUICHE WITH POTATO CRUST

**5 medium (1kg) potatoes,
    peeled, chopped**
¼ cup (20g) grated parmesan cheese
1 teaspoon dry mustard
60g butter, melted
**¾ cup (105g) plain flour,
    approximately**
1 egg, lightly beaten
FILLING
1 tablespoon olive oil
1 small (80g) onion, chopped
1 teaspoon chopped fresh rosemary
1 tablespoon chopped fresh parsley
**100g shitake mushrooms,
    finely chopped**
½ cup (125ml) cream
2 eggs, lightly beaten
75g soft goats' cheese

Grease 25cm pie plate, lightly dust with a little flour; shake away excess flour. Boil, steam or microwave potatoes until tender; drain, mash, cool. Stir in cheese, mustard, butter and enough flour to mix to a firm dough. Press potato dough over base and side of prepared plate, decorate edge using a fork; refrigerate 2 hours or until potato case is firm.

Brush potato case with egg. Bake in hot oven 15 minutes or until lightly browned. Pour filling into potato case, bake in moderate oven 25 minutes or until filling is set. Stand 10 minutes before serving. Serve warm or cold.
Filling: Heat oil in pan, add onion and rosemary, cook, stirring, until onion is soft. Stir in parsley and mushrooms, cook further 5 minutes or until mushrooms are tender; cool 5 minutes. Whisk cream, eggs and cheese in small bowl until smooth. Add mushroom mixture to egg mixture; mix well.

Serves 6.

■ Recipe can be made a day ahead.
■ Storage: Covered, in refrigerator.
■ Freeze: Not suitable.
■ Microwave: Potatoes and
    filling suitable.

LAMB HOT POTS WITH BUTTERY POTATO

2 tablespoons vegetable oil
1kg diced lamb
1 tablespoon vegetable oil, extra
1 large (200g) onion, sliced
2 cloves garlic, crushed
½ cup (125ml) dry red wine
1½ cups (375ml) beef stock
2 tablespoons tomato paste
1 tablespoon chopped fresh thyme
1 tablespoon chopped fresh oregano
425g can tomatoes
1 teaspoon sugar
1 tablespoon plain flour
2 tablespoons water
**1 medium (400g) kumara,
    peeled, chopped**
200g button mushrooms, halved
**4 medium (800g) new potatoes,
    thinly sliced**
30g butter, melted

Heat oil in pan, add lamb in batches, cook until well browned all over; remove from pan. Heat extra oil in same pan, add onion and garlic, cook, stirring, until onion is soft. Add wine, stock, paste, herbs, undrained crushed tomatoes and sugar, simmer, uncovered, 5 minutes.

Return lamb to pan, simmer, covered, 30 minutes. Remove lid, simmer further 30 minutes. Stir in blended flour and water, stir over high heat until mixture boils and thickens. Stir in kumara and mushrooms. Spoon mixture into 4 ovenproof dishes (2 cup/500ml capacity), place potato slices on top, brush with butter. Bake in moderate oven for about 50 minutes or until browned.

Serves 4.

■ Recipe can be made a day ahead.
■ Storage: Covered, in refrigerator.
■ Freeze: Suitable.
■ Microwave: Not suitable.

LEFT: From left: Double Potato and Chicken Cheesecake, Creamy Shitake Quiche with Potato Crust.
RIGHT: Lamb Hot Pots with Buttery Potato.

Left: Plate and bowl from Accoutrement. Right: Dish from Accoutrement.

WHOLEMEAL PARATHAS WITH SPICY MINCE FILLING

1½ cups (240g) wholemeal plain flour
½ cup (75g) white plain flour
30g ghee
⅔ cup (160ml) water, approximately
ghee for shallow-frying

SPICY MINCE FILLING
3 medium (600g) old potatoes, peeled, chopped
2 tablespoons plain yogurt
1 tablespoon vegetable oil
1 medium (150g) onion, finely chopped
1 clove garlic, crushed
2 teaspoons ground cumin
2 teaspoons ground coriander
1 tablespoon mild curry powder
½ teaspoon garam masala
250g minced pork and veal
1 teaspoon lemon juice

CUCUMBER YOGURT
3 small (390g) green cucumbers
2 cups (500ml) plain yogurt
1 tablespoon chopped fresh coriander
1 tablespoon chopped fresh mint

Sift flours into bowl, rub in ghee (or process flours and ghee until mixture resembles coarse breadcrumbs). Add enough water to make ingredients cling together (or process until ingredients just come together). Knead on lightly floured surface about 5 minutes or until smooth.

Divide dough into 16 portions, roll into 14cm rounds. Spread spicy mince filling over half the rounds, brush edges with water, top with remaining rounds, press edges together to seal. Using a rolling pin, gently roll rounds to 15cm diameter.

Shallow-fry rounds in hot ghee until browned and heated through; drain on absorbent paper. Serve parathas with cucumber yogurt.

Spicy Mince Filling: Boil, steam or microwave potatoes until tender; drain, rinse under cold water, drain. Mash potatoes, stir in yogurt.

Heat oil in pan, add onion and garlic, cook, stirring, until onion is soft. Add spices, cook, stirring, about 3 minutes or until fragrant. Add mince, cook, stirring, until well browned; stir in juice; cool. Combine potato mixture and mince mixture in bowl; mix well.

Cucumber Yogurt: Cut cucumbers in half lengthways. Scoop out seeds, chop cucumber. Combine cucumbers with yogurt and herbs in bowl; mix well.

Makes 8.

■ Filling and cucumber yogurt can be made a day ahead.
■ Storage: Covered, separately, in refrigerator.
■ Freeze: Not suitable.
■ Microwave: Potatoes suitable.

PAN-FRIED FISH WITH CRUNCHY POTATO TOPPING

5 baby (200g) new potatoes, thinly sliced
vegetable oil for shallow-frying
30g butter
1 tablespoon vegetable oil, extra
1 clove garlic, crushed
4 (600g) white fish fillets
½ teaspoon lemon pepper seasoning
2 teaspoons chopped fresh dill

CREAMY DILL SAUCE
½ cup (125ml) sour cream
¼ cup (60ml) cream
1 clove garlic, crushed
20g butter, chopped
1 tablespoon chopped fresh dill

Shallow-fry potatoes in hot oil in batches until golden; drain on absorbent paper. Sprinkle potatoes lightly with salt, if desired.

Meanwhile, heat butter and extra oil in pan, add garlic and fish, cook until lightly browned on both sides and tender.

Sprinkle fish with lemon pepper seasoning and dill, top with potatoes. Serve with creamy dill sauce.

Creamy Dill Sauce: Combine creams and garlic in small pan, bring to boil, simmer, uncovered, for 1 minute; whisk in butter and dill.

Serves 4.

■ Recipe best made just before serving.
■ Freeze: Not suitable.
■ Microwave: Not suitable.

ABOVE: Pan-Fried Fish with Crunchy Potato Topping.
RIGHT: From back: Vegetable Curry with Baby New Potatoes, Wholemeal Parathas with Spicy Mince Filling.

Right: China from Villeroy & Boch; metal dish and gold wooden tray from Parker's of Turramurra.

VEGETABLE CURRY WITH BABY NEW POTATOES

1 tablespoon vegetable oil
1 large (200g) onion, sliced
2 cloves garlic, crushed
3 teaspoons ground coriander
1 tablespoon ground cumin
½ teaspoon ground turmeric
¼ teaspoon chilli powder
1 tablespoon garam masala
12 baby (480g) new potatoes, quartered
2 x 425g cans tomatoes

½ teaspoon sugar
½ small (500g) cauliflower, chopped
1 cup (125g) frozen peas
1 cup (250ml) cream
2 tablespoons chopped fresh coriander

Heat oil in pan, add onion and garlic, cook, stirring, until onion is soft; add ground spices, cook, stirring, until fragrant. Add potatoes, cook 5 minutes, stirring occasionally. Add undrained crushed tomatoes and sugar, simmer, covered, 15 minutes. Add cauliflower, cook, covered, 5 minutes; add peas, cook until all vegetables are tender. Just before serving, stir in cream and sprinkle curry with fresh coriander.

Serves 4.

■ Recipe can be made, without cream, 2 days ahead.
■ Storage: Covered, in refrigerator.
■ Freeze: Not suitable.
■ Microwave: Suitable.

CHICKEN AND POTATO PIE

10 baby (400g) new potatoes, halved
1 medium (200g) red pepper
1 medium (200g) yellow pepper
2 tablespoons vegetable oil
800g chicken thigh fillets, chopped
1 tablespoon vegetable oil, extra
2 medium (700g) leeks, sliced
2 cloves garlic, crushed
1 tablespoon cornflour
½ cup (125ml) chicken stock
¼ cup (60ml) sour cream
2 tablespoons chopped fresh basil
1 egg, lightly beaten
1 sheet ready-rolled puff pastry

Boil, steam or microwave potatoes until just tender; drain, cool. Quarter peppers, remove seeds and membranes. Grill peppers, skin side up, until skin blisters and blackens. Peel away skin, slice peppers.

Heat oil in pan, add chicken in batches, cook, stirring, until well browned; drain on absorbent paper. Heat extra oil in pan, add leeks and garlic, cook, stirring, until leeks are soft. Add chicken, potatoes, blended cornflour and stock to pan, cook, stirring, until mixture boils and thickens. Stir in cream, peppers and basil; cool.

Spoon mixture into deep 25cm ovenproof dish (1.75 litre/7 cup capacity). Brush rim of dish with egg, place pastry over filling, trim edge. Brush pastry with egg, cut 3 slits in pastry. Bake in moderately hot oven about 30 minutes or until pie is golden brown.

Serves 6.

- Recipe can be prepared a day ahead.
- Storage: Covered, in refrigerator.
- Freeze: Not suitable.
- Microwave: Potatoes suitable.

VEGETARIAN SHEPHERD'S PIE

2 tablespoons vegetable oil
2 medium (300g) onions, sliced
2 cloves garlic, crushed
1 tablespoon mild curry powder
2 x 425g cans tomatoes
3 cups (300g) chopped cauliflower
3½ cups (300g) chopped broccoli
2 medium (240g) carrots, sliced
2 medium (250g) parsnips, sliced
2 tablespoons mild sweet chilli sauce

POTATO TOPPING
6 medium (1.2kg) potatoes, peeled
2 tablespoons sour cream
40g butter

Heat oil in pan, add onions and garlic, cook, stirring, until onions are soft. Add curry powder, cook, stirring, until fragrant. Stir in undrained crushed tomatoes with remaining ingredients, simmer, uncovered, 10 minutes or until mixture thickens and vegetables are tender; cool 10 minutes. Spoon vegetable mixture into ovenproof dish (2.5 litre/10 cup capacity), spread with potato topping. Bake in moderately hot oven about 25 minutes or until browned and hot.

Potato Topping: Boil, steam or microwave potatoes until tender; drain. Mash well with cream and butter.

Serves 6.

- ◾ Recipe can be made a day ahead.
- ◾ Storage: Covered, in refrigerator.
- ◾ Freeze: Not suitable.
- ◾ Microwave: Potatoes suitable.

LEFT: From back: Chicken and Potato Pie, Vegetarian Shepherd's Pie.
BELOW: Fish with Red Wine Sauce and Kumara Straws.

FISH WITH RED WINE SAUCE AND KUMARA STRAWS

2 tablespoons vegetable oil
40g butter
4 (1kg) boneless white fish fillets

RED WINE SAUCE
2 tablespoons dry red wine
2 tablespoons red wine vinegar
2 French shallots, finely chopped
300ml cream
2 tablespoons chopped fresh chives
1 teaspoon dry red wine, extra

KUMARA STRAWS
2 medium (800g) kumara, peeled
vegetable oil for deep-frying

Heat oil and butter in large frying pan, add fish, cook until lightly browned on both sides. Serve fish with red wine sauce and kumara straws.

Red Wine Sauce: Combine wine, wine vinegar and shallots in small pan over heat, simmer, uncovered, until reduced to 2 tablespoons of liquid. Stir in cream, simmer, uncovered, until mixture is reduced to ¾ cup (180ml). Stir in chives and extra wine.

Kumara Straws: Cut kumara into 2mm slices, then into 2mm strips. Just before serving, deep-fry kumara in hot oil in batches until lightly browned and crisp; drain on absorbent paper.

Serves 4.

- ◾ Red wine sauce can be made 3 hours ahead. Fish and kumara best cooked close to serving.
- ◾ Storage: Sauce, covered, in refrigerator.
- ◾ Freeze: Not suitable.
- ◾ Microwave: Not suitable.

MUSTARD CREAM CHICKEN WITH POTATO HASH

1 tablespoon vegetable oil
1 clove garlic, crushed
4 chicken breast fillets
¾ cup (180ml) dry white wine
1 tablespoon chopped fresh basil
2 teaspoons French mustard
½ cup (125ml) cream
3 green shallots, sliced
1 teaspoon cornflour
2 teaspoons water

POTATO HASH
2 large (600g) old potatoes, peeled, grated
1 egg, lightly beaten
1 tablespoon plain flour
1 tablespoon chopped fresh parsley
½ teaspoon seasoned pepper
2 tablespoons vegetable oil

Heat oil in pan, add garlic and chicken, cook until browned all over. Add wine, basil and mustard, simmer, covered, 15 minutes. Stir in cream, shallots and blended cornflour and water, cook, stirring, until mixture boils and thickens. Serve chicken sliced with potato hash.

Potato Hash: Squeeze excess moisture from potatoes, combine with egg, flour, parsley and pepper in bowl; mix well. Heat oil in pan, add quarter of the potato mixture; flatten and shape into a round. Cook slowly until browned underneath, turn, brown other side; drain on absorbent paper, keep warm. Repeat with remaining potato mixture.

Serves 4.

■ Recipe best made close to serving.
■ Freeze: Not suitable.
■ Microwave: Not suitable.

FRESH SALMON CAKES WITH HERB MAYONNAISE

1 cup (250ml) water
2 cups (500ml) dry white wine
1 stick celery, chopped
1 medium (120g) carrot, chopped
½ teaspoon black peppercorns
500g Atlantic salmon cutlets
2 large (600g) potatoes, peeled
pinch saffron strands
2 green shallots, chopped
2 cloves garlic, crushed
1 tablespoon drained capers, chopped
plain flour
2 eggs, lightly beaten
½ cup (50g) packaged breadcrumbs
¼ cup (30g) packaged ground almonds
40g butter
1 tablespoon olive oil

HERB MAYONNAISE
⅔ cup (160ml) mayonnaise
¼ cup (60ml) thickened cream
1 teaspoon Dijon mustard
1 tablespoon chopped fresh parsley
1 tablespoon chopped fresh chives

Combine water, wine, celery, carrot and peppercorns in large pan, bring to boil, reduce heat; add salmon. Cook gently, uncovered, about 10 minutes or until salmon is tender; drain on absorbent paper. Strain and reserve liquid; discard pulp.

Cut potatoes into 1cm cubes. Place reserved liquid in pan, add saffron and potatoes, simmer, uncovered, about 10 minutes or until potatoes are tender; drain, cool. Mash two-thirds of the potatoes. Remove skin and bones from salmon, flake salmon gently into small pieces. Combine all potatoes, salmon, shallots, garlic and capers in bowl; mix well.

Divide mixture into 8 portions; shape into 8cm cakes. Gently toss cakes in flour, shake away excess flour. Dip into eggs, then combined breadcrumbs and nuts. Refrigerate 30 minutes.

Heat butter and oil in pan, add salmon cakes, cook, turning once, until well browned. Serve with herb mayonnaise.

Herb Mayonnaise: Combine all ingredients in bowl; mix well.

Makes 8.

■ Recipe can be prepared a day ahead.
■ Storage: Covered, in refrigerator.
■ Freeze: Suitable.
■ Microwave: Salmon and potatoes suitable.

LEFT: Mustard Cream Chicken with Potato Hash.
RIGHT: From back: Fresh Salmon Cakes with Herb Mayonnaise, Sardine Croquettes with Yogurt Sauce.

SARDINE CROQUETTES WITH YOGURT SAUCE

5 medium (1kg) old potatoes, peeled, chopped
30g butter
2 teaspoons tomato paste
1 tablespoon chopped fresh basil
2 green shallots, chopped
105g can sardines, drained, chopped
1 egg yolk
1 teaspoon lemon juice
plain flour
2 eggs, lightly beaten
packaged breadcrumbs
vegetable oil for deep-frying

YOGURT SAUCE
1 cup (250ml) plain yogurt
1 tablespoon tomato sauce
1 tablespoon chopped fresh basil
few drops Tabasco sauce
¼ teaspoon Worcestershire sauce

Boil, steam or microwave potatoes until tender, rinse under cold water; drain. Mash potatoes with butter. Add paste, basil, shallots, sardines, egg yolk and juice; mix well. Drop ⅓ cup quantities of mixture into flour, shape into croquettes, shake away excess flour. Dip into eggs, then breadcrumbs. Deep-fry croquettes in hot oil until golden brown; drain on absorbent paper. Serve with yogurt sauce.

Yogurt Sauce: Combine all ingredients in bowl; mix well.

Makes 8.

- ■ Recipe can be prepared a day ahead.
- ■ Storage: Covered, in refrigerator.
- ■ Freeze: Uncooked croquettes suitable.
- ■ Microwave: Potatoes suitable.

41

SPINACH, POTATO AND FETA CHEESE PIE

2 medium (400g) new potatoes,
    peeled
60g butter
1 medium (350g) leek, sliced
1 clove garlic, crushed
½ teaspoon cumin seeds
250g packet frozen spinach, thawed,
    well drained
100g feta cheese, crumbled
1 tablespoon chopped fresh
    coriander
8 sheets fillo pastry
50g butter, melted, extra

Grease 22cm round ovenproof pie dish
(1 litre/4 cup capacity). Cut potatoes into
2cm pieces. Boil, steam or microwave
potatoes until tender; drain, rinse.

Heat butter in pan, add leek, garlic and
seeds, cook, stirring, until leek is soft. Add
spinach, cook, stirring, about 3 minutes or
until liquid is evaporated. Stir in potatoes,
cheese and coriander; mix well.

Layer 2 sheets of pastry together,
brushing each with a little of the extra butter. Fold layered sheets in half lengthways, place in prepared dish with edges
overhanging. Repeat with remaining
pastry and extra butter, overlapping strips
around dish until covered.

Spoon potato mixture into dish, fold
overhanging edges back over filling and
gather in centre. Brush all over with extra
butter, bake in moderate oven about 30
minutes or until browned and hot.

Serves 4 to 6.

■ Recipe can be prepared a day ahead.
■ Storage: Covered, in refrigerator.
■ Freeze: Not suitable.
■ Microwave: Potatoes suitable.

ABOVE: Spinach, Potato and Feta
Cheese Pie.
TOP RIGHT: Sherried Vegetable Hot Pot
with Risoni.
RIGHT: Cheesy Potato Pizza.

Above: Tea-towel from Accoutrement.

CHEESY POTATO PIZZA

3 medium (600g) old potatoes,
    peeled, chopped
20g butter
1/3 cup (25g) finely grated
    parmesan cheese
1 egg, lightly beaten
1/3 cup (80ml) tomato paste
1 medium (130g) tomato, seeded,
    thinly sliced
1½ cups (150g) grated
    mozzarella cheese
8 slices (80g) salami
40g button mushrooms, thinly sliced
2 teaspoons chopped fresh oregano
1 small (80g) onion, sliced

Grease 24cm round loose-base flan tin.
Boil, steam or microwave potatoes until
tender; mash with butter, parmesan
cheese and egg until smooth; cool.
Spread potato mixture over base of
prepared tin, refrigerate 30 minutes or
until slightly firm.

Gently spread tomato paste over potato
base, top with tomato slices, 1 cup (100g)
of the mozzarella cheese, salami, mushrooms, oregano, onion and remaining
cheese. Bake in moderately hot oven 30
minutes or until lightly browned and hot.

Serves 4 to 6.

■ Recipe can be prepared a day ahead.
■ Storage: Covered, in refrigerator.
■ Freeze: Uncooked pizza suitable.
■ Microwave: Potatoes suitable.

SHERRIED VEGETABLE HOT POT WITH RISONI

1.4kg butternut pumpkin
1 cup (250ml) vegetable stock
10 baby (400g) new potatoes
1/4 cup (60ml) olive oil
1 teaspoon ground turmeric
1 teaspoon paprika
1/2 cup (100g) risoni
1 tablespoon olive oil, extra
1 large (500g) leek, chopped
5 cups (400g) shredded cabbage
2 cups (500ml) vegetable stock, extra
1/4 cup (60ml) dry sherry
1/4 cup chopped fresh chives

Peel pumpkin, remove seeds, chop
pumpkin into 3cm pieces. Boil, steam or
microwave half the pumpkin until tender,
blend or process with stock until smooth;
cool. Cover pumpkin puree, refrigerate
until required.

Place remaining pumpkin, potatoes, oil,
turmeric and paprika in bowl; mix well.
Spread potato mixture into baking dish,
bake in moderately hot oven about 1 hour
or until vegetables are lightly browned and
tender, stirring halfway during cooking time.

Add risoni to pan of boiling water, boil,
uncovered, until tender; drain, cool.

Heat extra oil in large pan, add leek,
cook, covered, over low heat about 5
minutes or until tender, stirring occasionally. Stir in cabbage, reserved pumpkin
puree, extra stock and sherry, simmer, uncovered, 10 minutes or until cabbage is
tender. Stir in potato mixture, risoni and
chives, cook, stirring, until heated
through.

Serves 6.

■ Recipe best made close to serving.
■ Freeze: Not suitable.
■ Microwave: Suitable.

MEATBALLS IN TOMATO THYME SAUCE

1 tablespoon olive oil
1 large (200g) onion, chopped
2 medium (400g) old potatoes, peeled, grated
500g minced beef
1 cup (100g) packaged breadcrumbs
1 egg, lightly beaten
1 tablespoon chopped fresh thyme
1 teaspoon grated lemon rind
vegetable oil for deep-frying

TOMATO THYME SAUCE
2 tablespoons olive oil
2 medium (300g) onions, sliced
2 x 425g cans tomatoes
2 teaspoons beef stock powder
2 tablespoons chopped fresh thyme
1 teaspoon sugar

Heat olive oil in pan, add onion, cook, stirring, until onion is soft; add potatoes, cook, stirring, 5 minutes; cool 10 minutes. Combine potato mixture, mince, breadcrumbs, egg, thyme and rind in bowl; mix well. Using floured hands, roll level tablespoons of mixture into balls, shake away excess flour. Refrigerate meatballs 30 minutes.

Deep-fry meatballs in batches in hot vegetable oil until browned; drain on absorbent paper. Add meatballs to tomato thyme sauce, simmer, uncovered, about 5 minutes or until heated through.

Tomato Thyme Sauce: Heat oil in pan, add onions, cook, stirring, until onions are soft. Stir in undrained crushed tomatoes and stock powder, simmer, uncovered, about 10 minutes or until slightly thickened. Stir in thyme and sugar.

Serves 4 to 6.

- Recipe can be made a day ahead.
- Storage: Covered, in refrigerator.
- Freeze: Meatballs suitable.
- Microwave: Not suitable.

CREAMY PASTA WITH BABY POTATOES AND PROSCIUTTO

500g spaghetti pasta
8 baby (320g) new potatoes, quartered
2 medium (400g) red peppers
12 slices (120g) prosciutto
1 tablespoon olive oil
1 large (200g) onion, sliced
2 cloves garlic, crushed
2 medium (240g) zucchini, sliced
300ml sour cream
¼ cup (60ml) milk
1 tablespoon chopped fresh basil
2 teaspoons chopped fresh thyme
¼ cup (20g) grated parmesan cheese
⅓ cup (25g) flaked parmesan cheese, extra

Add pasta to large pan of boiling water, boil, uncovered, until pasta is just tender; drain. Boil, steam or microwave potatoes until just tender; cool.

Quarter peppers, remove seeds and membranes. Grill peppers, skin side up, until skin blisters and blackens. Peel skin, slice peppers into thin strips. Cut prosciutto into 1cm strips, grill half the prosciutto on greased oven tray until crisp; cool.

Heat oil in pan, add onion and garlic, cook, stirring, until onion is soft. Add potatoes and zucchini, cook, stirring, until potatoes are lightly browned and zucchini is tender. Add the ungrilled prosciutto and peppers, cook until heated through. Remove half this vegetable mixture from pan; reserve.

Add cream, milk, herbs and grated cheese to pan, simmer, uncovered, 2 minutes. Add cream mixture to pasta in bowl; mix well. Serve pasta topped with reserved vegetable mixture, grilled prosciutto and extra parmesan cheese.

Serves 4 to 6.

- Recipe best made just before serving.
- Freeze: Not suitable.
- Microwave: Pasta and potatoes suitable.

LEFT: Meatballs in Tomato Thyme Sauce.
RIGHT: From back: Italian Veal and Potato with Tomato Sauce, Creamy Pasta with Baby Potatoes and Prosciutto.

ITALIAN VEAL AND POTATO WITH TOMATO SAUCE

1 large (300g) potato, peeled, chopped
½ bunch (325g) English spinach
30g butter
1 tablespoon olive oil
4 veal steaks
1 clove garlic, crushed
½ teaspoon seasoned pepper
⅓ cup (25g) grated parmesan cheese

TOMATO SAUCE
2 teaspoons olive oil
1 clove garlic, crushed
410g can tomato puree

½ cup (75g) pimiento-stuffed green olives, sliced
¼ cup (60ml) dry red wine
1 tablespoon chopped fresh oregano
1 teaspoon sugar

Grease ovenproof dish (2.25 litre/9 cup capacity). Boil, steam or microwave potato until tender; drain, cut potato into 5mm slices. Boil, steam or microwave spinach until just tender; drain, rinse.

Heat butter and oil in pan, add veal and garlic, cook until browned all over. Place veal into prepared dish, top with spinach and potato slices, sprinkle with pepper and half the cheese. Pour tomato sauce

around veal, sprinkle veal with remaining cheese. Cover, bake in moderately hot oven 20 minutes, remove cover, bake further 10 minutes or until heated through.
Tomato Sauce: Heat oil in pan, add remaining ingredients, simmer, uncovered, 10 minutes.

Serves 4.

- Recipe can be prepared a day ahead.
- Storage: Covered, in refrigerator.
- Freeze: Not suitable.
- Microwave: Potato and spinach suitable.

45

SHEPHERD'S PIE WITH KUMARA TOPPING

500g lamb fillets
1½ tablespoons vegetable oil
1 large (200g) onion, chopped
2 cloves garlic, crushed
2 x 425g cans tomatoes
1 tablespoon seeded mustard
2 teaspoons chopped fresh thyme
1 tablespoon chopped fresh oregano
1 tablespoon chopped fresh parsley
250g button mushrooms, chopped
1 tablespoon cornflour
2 tablespoons water
½ cup (60g) frozen peas

KUMARA TOPPING
3 small (750g) kumara,
peeled, chopped
2 medium (400g) potatoes,
peeled, chopped
½ cup (40g) grated parmesan cheese
1 egg yolk
2 tablespoons cream

Cut lamb into 2cm pieces. Heat oil in pan, add lamb, onion and garlic, cook, stirring, until lamb is browned and onion is soft. Stir in undrained crushed tomatoes, mustard and herbs, simmer, uncovered, 15 minutes or until lamb is tender. Stir in mushrooms and blended cornflour and water, stir over heat until mixture boils and thickens; stir in peas.

Spoon mixture into ovenproof dish (2 litre/ 8 cup capacity). Spoon kumara topping into piping bag fitted with large star tube, gently pipe topping over lamb mixture. Bake in moderately hot oven about 30 minutes or until lightly browned.

Kumara Topping: Boil, steam or microwave kumara and potatoes until tender; mash with cheese, egg yolk and cream until smooth.

Serves 4.

- Recipe can be made a day ahead.
- Storage: Covered, in refrigerator.
- Freeze: Suitable.
- Microwave: Kumara and potatoes suitable.

BEEF, POTATO AND ROSEMARY RAGOUT

1kg chuck steak
1 medium (400g) kumara, peeled
1 tablespoon olive oil
2 bacon rashers, chopped
2 medium (300g) onions, chopped
2 cloves garlic, crushed
½ cup (125ml) tomato puree
1 cup (250ml) beef stock
⅓ cup (80ml) dry red wine
10cm sprig fresh rosemary
1 tablespoon Worcestershire sauce
12 baby (480g) new potatoes,
quartered
2 tablespoons plain flour
¾ cup (180ml) water

Cut steak and kumara into 3cm pieces. Heat oil in pan, cook steak in batches, stirring, until well browned. Add bacon, onions and garlic to steak in pan, cook, stirring, until onions are soft and liquid has evaporated.

Stir in puree, stock, wine, rosemary and sauce, simmer, covered, about 1 hour or until beef is only just tender. Stir in kumara, potatoes and blended flour and water, stir over heat until mixture boils and thickens; simmer, uncovered, further 20 minutes or until vegetables and steak are tender. Discard rosemary.

Serves 4 to 6.

- Recipe can be made a day ahead.
- Storage: Covered, in refrigerator.
- Freeze: Suitable.
- Microwave: Not suitable.

POTATO LENTIL BURGERS WITH CHILLI CREAM

You will need to cook 2 large (600g) old potatoes for this recipe.

1 cup (200g) red lentils
1 tablespoon olive oil
2 medium (300g) onions, sliced
1 clove garlic, crushed
½ cup (80g) pine nuts
1½ cups cold mashed potato
2 tablespoons chopped fresh basil
1 tablespoon seeded mustard
½ cup (40g) grated parmesan cheese
1 egg yolk
1 cup (70g) stale breadcrumbs
½ cup (50g) packaged breadcrumbs
vegetable oil for shallow-frying
6 hamburger buns
150g snow pea sprouts

CHILLI CREAM
⅔ cup (160ml) sour cream
2 tablespoons mild sweet chilli sauce

Add lentils to pan of boiling water, boil, uncovered, about 10 minutes or until tender; drain. Heat olive oil in pan, add onions, garlic and nuts, stir over heat until onions are soft and nuts lightly browned.

Combine lentils, potato, onion mixture, basil, mustard, cheese, egg yolk and stale breadcrumbs in bowl; mix well. Shape mixture into 6 patties, toss in packaged breadcrumbs; refrigerate patties 1 hour or until firm. Shallow-fry patties in hot oil until lightly browned on both sides and heated through; drain. Serve patties on toasted buns with sprouts and chilli cream.

Chilli Cream: Combine both ingredients in bowl; mix well.

Serves 6.

- Patties can be made a day ahead.
- Storage: Covered, in refrigerator.
- Freeze: Patties suitable.
- Microwave: Potatoes and lentils suitable.

LEFT: From back: Beef, Potato and Rosemary Ragout, Shepherd's Pie with Kumara Topping.
RIGHT: Potato Lentil Burgers with Chilli Cream.

Left: Cloth from Morris Home & Garden Wares.

BOUILLABAISSE WITH POTATO ROUILLE

We have adapted the traditional rouille into this delicious potato version; spread it on bread or fish.

500g medium uncooked prawns
500g snapper fillets
300g small mussels
2 tablespoons olive oil
2 large (400g) onions, sliced
2 cloves garlic, crushed
425g can tomatoes
½ cup (125ml) tomato paste
2 tablespoons chopped fresh thyme
1 small (450g) fennel bulb, sliced
¼ teaspoon saffron powder
5 medium (1kg) old potatoes, peeled, sliced

FISH STOCK
2 (1kg) snapper fish heads
2 sticks celery, chopped
1 medium (150g) onion, chopped
1 medium (120g) carrot, chopped
2 sprigs fresh thyme
2 bay leaves
8 black peppercorns
3 litres (12 cups) water

POTATO ROUILLE
2 cloves garlic, crushed
½ teaspoon tomato paste
¼ cup (60ml) olive oil
pinch hot chilli powder

Shell and devein prawns, leaving tails intact. Cut fish into 2cm pieces. Scrub mussels, remove beards.

Heat oil in large pan, add onions and garlic, cook, stirring, until onions are soft. Add undrained crushed tomatoes, paste, thyme and fennel, cook, stirring, 3 minutes. Add hot fish stock, saffron and potatoes, simmer, uncovered, about 15 minutes or until potatoes are just tender.

Reserve quarter of the potatoes and ¼ cup (60ml) of the fish stock for potato rouille. Just before serving, add seafood to bouillabaisse, cook, uncovered, 5 minutes or until seafood is cooked through. Serve bouillabaisse with potato rouille.

Fish Stock: Place all ingredients in large pan, simmer, uncovered, 20 minutes, skimming when necessary. Carefully strain mixture; you need 2.5 litres (10 cups) of stock for this recipe. Discard fish heads and vegetables.

Potato Rouille: Mash reserved potatoes, push through a fine sieve, add garlic and paste, stir until smooth. Gradually add oil in a thin stream, stirring constantly, then gradually stir in enough reserved stock to form a soft paste. Stir in chilli powder.

Serves 6.

- Recipe can be prepared a day ahead.
- Storage: Covered, in refrigerator.
- Freeze: Stock suitable.
- Microwave: Not suitable.

KOFTA

3 medium (600g) old potatoes, peeled, chopped
750g minced lamb
½ cup (35g) stale breadcrumbs
1 egg, lightly beaten
¼ cup (40g) pine nuts, toasted
1 teaspoon cumin seeds
½ teaspoon ground cinnamon
½ teaspoon ground cardamom
¼ cup (40g) raisins, chopped
2 tablespoons olive oil

TOMATO SAUCE
425g can tomatoes
20g butter
1 medium (150g) onion, chopped
1 clove garlic, crushed
1 teaspoon ground cumin
1 tablespoon chopped fresh parsley

Boil, steam or microwave potatoes until tender; drain, mash. Combine potatoes, mince, breadcrumbs, egg, nuts, seeds, cinnamon, cardamom and raisins in bowl; mix well. Divide mixture into 24 portions, shape into sausages about 9cm long, thread onto skewers.

Heat oil in pan, cook kofta in batches until well browned and cooked through. Serve with tomato sauce, and sprinkled with extra pine nuts, if desired.

Tomato Sauce: Blend or process tomatoes until smooth. Heat butter in pan, add onion and garlic, cook, stirring, until onion is soft. Add pureed tomatoes, cumin and parsley, cook, stirring, until hot.

Serves 6.

- Recipe can be prepared a day ahead.
- Storage: Covered, separately, in refrigerator.
- Freeze: Suitable.
- Microwave: Potatoes suitable.

POTATO, LAMB AND BURGHUL CROQUETTES

2 medium (400g) potatoes, peeled, chopped
¼ cup (40g) burghul
2 teaspoons vegetable oil
1 clove garlic, crushed
250g minced lamb
1 small (80g) onion, chopped
1 medium (120g) carrot, grated
1 egg, lightly beaten
1 tablespoon chopped fresh thyme
1 teaspoon ground cumin
⅓ cup (35g) packaged breadcrumbs, approximately
⅓ cup (80ml) vegetable oil, extra

YOGURT MINT SAUCE
½ cup (125ml) plain yogurt
1 tablespoon chopped fresh mint
1 teaspoon sugar
1 teaspoon lemon juice

Boil, steam or microwave potatoes until tender; drain, mash. Place burghul in heatproof bowl, cover with boiling water, stand 15 minutes. Drain burghul, rinse under cold water, drain well. Pat dry with absorbent paper.

Heat oil in pan, add garlic, mince, onion and carrot, cook, stirring, until mince is browned. Stir in potato, burghul, egg, thyme and cumin; mix well. Divide mixture into 12 portions, shape into croquettes, roll in breadcrumbs. Refrigerate 30 minutes or until firm.

Heat extra oil in pan, cook croquettes in batches until browned; drain on absorbent paper. Serve with yogurt mint sauce.
Yogurt Mint Sauce: Combine all ingredients in bowl: mix well.

Serves 4.

- Uncooked croquettes and sauce can be prepared a day ahead.
- Storage: Covered, separately, in refrigerator.
- Freeze: Uncooked croquettes suitable.
- Microwave: Potatoes suitable.

LEFT: Bouillabaisse with Potato Rouille.
RIGHT: From left: Kofta, Potato, Lamb and Burghul Croquettes.

Left: Bowls from Barbara's Storehouse.
Right: Plates from Ventura Design; terracotta planter from Parker's of Turramurra.

THAI-STYLE POTATO CURRY WITH PRAWNS

4 medium (800g) potatoes,
  peeled, chopped
500g medium uncooked prawns
1 tablespoon vegetable oil
1 tablespoon bottled red curry paste
1 medium (150g) onion, chopped
1½ cups (375ml) coconut milk
1 tablespoon fish sauce
1 teaspoon grated lime rind
1 tablespoon lime juice
2 medium (260g) tomatoes,
  peeled, chopped
1 tablespoon shredded fresh basil

Boil, steam or microwave potatoes until
tender. Shell and devein prawns, leaving
tails intact. Heat oil in pan, add curry
paste, cook, stirring, about 1 minute or
until fragrant. Add onion, cook, stirring,
until onion is soft. Add coconut milk,
sauce, rind, juice and tomatoes, bring to
boil. Add prawns, potatoes and basil, cook
gently, stirring occasionally, about 5
minutes or until prawns are tender.

Serves 4.

■ Recipe best made just before serving.
■ Freeze: Not suitable.
■ Microwave: Suitable.

CHEESY VEGETABLE MOUSSAKA

1 large (500g) eggplant
coarse cooking salt
¼ cup (60ml) olive oil
40g butter
2 large (600g) old potatoes,
  peeled, thinly sliced
2 tablespoons olive oil, extra
4 cloves garlic, crushed
2 medium (300g) onions, chopped
2 medium (240g) zucchini, grated
2 medium (240g) carrots, grated
425g can tomatoes
150g button mushrooms, sliced
1 tablespoon tomato paste
¼ cup (60ml) dry red wine
1 teaspoon sugar
⅓ cup (40g) grated tasty
  cheddar cheese

CHEESE SAUCE
40g butter
¼ cup (35g) plain flour
1¾ cups (430ml) milk
1 cup (80g) grated parmesan cheese
1 egg, lightly beaten

Grease shallow ovenproof dish (2.5 litre/
10 cup capacity). Cut eggplant into 5mm
slices, place slices on wire rack (or in
colander), sprinkle with salt, stand 30
minutes. Rinse eggplant under cold
water; drain on absorbent paper. Place
slices in single layer on oven trays, grill on
both sides until lightly browned; drain on
absorbent paper.

Heat oil and butter in pan, add potatoes
in batches, cook until well browned on
both sides; drain on absorbent paper.
Heat extra oil in pan, add garlic and

onions, cook, stirring, until onions are soft. Add zucchini and carrots, cook, stirring, 5 minutes. Stir in undrained crushed tomatoes, mushrooms, paste, wine and sugar, simmer, uncovered, about 20 minutes or until thickened. Place half the eggplant over base of prepared dish, top with half the potatoes and half the tomato mixture. Repeat with remaining eggplant, potatoes and tomato mixture. Top with cheese sauce, sprinkle with cheese. Bake in moderately hot oven about 25 minutes or until browned and heated through.

Cheese Sauce: Heat butter in pan, add flour, stir until bubbling. Remove from heat, gradually stir in milk, stir over heat until mixture boils and thickens. Remove from heat, stir in cheese, cool 5 minutes. Stir in egg; stir until smooth.

Serves 6.

- ▪ Recipe can be made 2 days ahead.
- ▪ Storage: Covered, in refrigerator.
- ▪ Freeze: Not suitable.
- ▪ Microwave: Not suitable.

ROAST LAMB WITH HERBED POTATOES

1 large (200g) onion, chopped
2 cloves garlic, crushed
1 tablespoon chopped fresh chives
1 tablespoon chopped fresh thyme
5 large (1.5kg) old potatoes,
   peeled, sliced
50g butter, chopped
1 cup (250ml) water
2kg leg of lamb
3 cloves garlic, extra

Grease 27cm x 34cm baking dish. Combine onion, crushed garlic and herbs in bowl; mix well. Place half of the potatoes over base of prepared dish, sprinkle with onion and herb mixture, top with remaining potatoes, dot with butter; add water. Bake in hot oven for 1 hour.

Cut 3 small slits in top of lamb, push a clove of extra garlic into each slit. Place lamb in baking dish on top of potatoes, bake in moderate oven further 1½ hours or until cooked as desired. Turn lamb halfway through cooking. Remove lamb from baking dish to heatproof plate, cover with foil, rest lamb 10 minutes before carving. Keep potatoes warm in oven while lamb is resting.

Serves 6.

- ▪ Recipe best cooked just before serving.
- ▪ Freeze: Not suitable.
- ▪ Microwave: Not suitable.

BELOW LEFT: Cheesy Vegetable Moussaka.
LEFT: Thai-Style Potato Curry with Prawns.
BELOW: Roast Lamb with Herbed Potatoes.

Below left: Dish from Villeroy & Boch; table and stone planter from FX Design. Below: Rug from Home & Garden on the Mall.

LAMB CASSEROLE WITH POTATOES AND ONIONS

2 x 1.5kg shoulders of lamb, boned
1 tablespoon vegetable oil
2 cloves garlic, crushed
2 teaspoons grated fresh ginger
2 sticks celery, chopped
1 tablespoon chopped fresh
    rosemary
½ teaspoon ground turmeric
1 cup (250ml) beef stock
1 cup (250ml) dry white wine
2 bay leaves
10 baby (400g) new potatoes
8 baby (200g) onions
1 tablespoon cornflour
1 tablespoon water
1 tablespoon chopped fresh parsley

Remove fat from lamb; cut lamb into 3cm cubes. Heat oil in pan, add garlic and ginger, cook lamb in batches until browned. Add celery, rosemary and turmeric to pan, cook, stirring, 2 minutes or until fragrant. Add stock, wine and bay leaves, simmer, covered, 45 minutes. Add potatoes and onions, simmer, covered, further 20 minutes or until potatoes are tender. Stir in blended cornflour and water, cook, stirring, until mixture boils and thickens; continue stirring further 1 minute. Discard bay leaves. Serve lamb casserole sprinkled with parsley.

Serves 4.

■ Recipe can be made a day ahead.
■ Storage: Covered, in refrigerator.
■ Freeze: Not suitable.
■ Microwave: Not suitable.

CHICKEN AND VEGETABLES IN CREAMY WINE SAUCE

8 (1.6kg) chicken thigh cutlets
1 tablespoon olive oil
2 cloves garlic, crushed
2 bacon rashers, chopped
1 medium (350g) leek, sliced
8 baby (200g) onions, peeled, halved
¼ cup (60ml) dry white wine
¾ cup (180ml) chicken stock
12 baby (480g) new potatoes
10 baby carrots
1 medium (125g) parsnip,
    peeled, sliced
1 tablespoon cornflour
2 tablespoons water
1 tablespoon chopped fresh chives
1 tablespoon chopped fresh thyme
½ cup (125ml) sour cream

Remove skin from chicken. Heat oil in pan, cook chicken in batches until well browned; drain on absorbent paper. Drain all but 1 tablespoon of juices from pan, add garlic, bacon, leek and onions, cook, stirring, until leek is soft.

Return chicken to pan, add wine, stock and vegetables. Simmer, covered, about 30 minutes or until vegetables and chicken are tender. Stir in blended cornflour and water, stir over heat until mixture boils and thickens. Stir in herbs and sour cream.

Serves 4.

- Recipe can be prepared several hours ahead.
- Storage: Covered, in refrigerator.
- Freeze: Suitable.
- Microwave: Suitable.

NACHOS IN POTATO BASKETS

**3 medium (600g) old potatoes,
    peeled, grated**
1 tablespoon plain flour
1 egg yolk
⅓ cup (80ml) vegetable oil
½ small iceberg lettuce, shredded
1 medium (130g) tomato, chopped
**½ cup (60g) grated tasty
    cheddar cheese**
⅓ cup (80ml) sour cream

FILLING
1 tablespoon vegetable oil
2 cloves garlic, crushed
**1 medium (150g) onion,
    finely chopped**
pinch cayenne pepper
½ teaspoon paprika
½ teaspoon celery salt
250g minced beef
425g can tomatoes
300g can Tomato Supreme
**310g can red kidney beans,
    drained, rinsed**

Combine potatoes, flour and egg yolk in bowl. Heat 1 tablespoon of the oil in pan, add quarter of the potato mixture, flatten to 14cm round, cook until browned underneath; turn, brown other side. Repeat with remaining oil and potato mixture.

Press warm potato rounds over upturned individual pie dishes (base measuring 9.5cm) on oven tray.

Bake in moderately hot oven about 20 minutes or until potato baskets are firm. Divide lettuce and tomato between potato baskets, top with filling, cheese and cream.
Filling: Heat oil in pan, add garlic, onion, pepper, paprika and salt, cook, stirring, until onion is soft. Add mince, cook, stirring, until lightly browned, stir in undrained crushed tomatoes, Tomato Supreme and beans, simmer, uncovered, 30 minutes or until mixture is thick.

Serves 4.

- Filling can be made a day ahead. Baskets best made just before serving.
- Storage: Filling, covered, in refrigerator.
- Freeze: Filling suitable.
- Microwave: Filling suitable.

*LEFT: From left: Lamb Casserole with Potatoes and Onions, Chicken and Vegetables in Creamy Wine Sauce.
BELOW: Nachos in Potato Baskets.*

Left: Pottery from Kenwick Galleries.

CHICKEN, PORK AND POTATOES IN PEANUT SAUCE

1kg chicken breast fillets
450g pork fillet
1/3 cup (80ml) olive oil
1 large (200g) onion, finely chopped
2 cloves garlic, crushed
1/4 teaspoon sambal oelek
2 teaspoons paprika
1 teaspoon ground cumin
2 medium (400g) old potatoes, peeled, chopped
3 cups (750ml) chicken stock
1/3 cup (50g) roasted unsalted peanuts
2 tablespoons smooth peanut butter
1/2 teaspoon grated lime rind
1 tablespoon lime juice
2 tablespoons chopped fresh coriander

Cut chicken and pork into 3cm pieces. Heat half the oil in pan, cook chicken and pork over high heat in batches until lightly browned; transfer to bowl.

Heat remaining oil in clean pan, add onion, garlic, sambal oelek, paprika and cumin, cook, stirring, until onion is soft. Add potatoes and 2 cups (500ml) of the stock to onion mixture, simmer, covered, 20 minutes or until potatoes are tender; cool to room temperature.

Blend or process potato mixture with remaining stock, peanuts and peanut butter until smooth. Return mixture to pan, add undrained chicken and pork, rind and juice, simmer, uncovered, 15 minutes or until chicken and pork are tender; stir in coriander.

Serves 6.

- ■ Recipe can be made a day ahead.
- ■ Storage: Covered, in refrigerator.
- ■ Freeze: Suitable.
- ■ Microwave: Not suitable.

GARLIC POTATOES WITH COUSCOUS-TOPPED CHICKEN

4 large (1.2kg) old potatoes, peeled
1/3 cup (80ml) olive oil
6 cloves garlic, crushed
1 tablespoon chopped fresh rosemary
8 (1.6kg) chicken thigh cutlets
1 tablespoon vegetable oil
1/2 cup (75g) couscous
1 teaspoon chicken stock powder
1 cup (250ml) boiling water
2 green shallots, finely chopped
1 medium (130g) tomato, finely chopped
1 tablespoon chopped fresh thyme
1/3 cup (65g) ricotta cheese
1 tablespoon lemon juice

Cut potatoes into 3cm pieces, place in baking dish, pour over combined olive oil, garlic and rosemary; mix well. Bake in moderately hot oven for 1 hour, turning occasionally.

Remove skin from chicken. Heat vegetable oil in pan, cook chicken in batches until lightly browned; drain on absorbent paper. Combine couscous, stock powder and water in bowl, stand 15 minutes or until water is absorbed. Combine couscous mixture with remaining ingredients in bowl; mix well. Divide couscous mixture into 8 portions; press a portion on top of each chicken cutlet.

Place chicken in baking dish with cooked potatoes, bake, uncovered, in moderate oven about 30 minutes or until chicken is tender.

Serves 4.

- Chicken can be prepared 3 hours ahead.
- Storage: Covered, in refrigerator.
- Freeze: Not suitable.
- Microwave: Not suitable.

POTATO PIZZA WITH CARAMELISED ONIONS

3 small (360g) old potatoes, peeled
2 tablespoons light olive oil
½ medium (75g) onion, chopped
1 clove garlic, crushed
1 cup (250ml) chicken stock
1½ cups (150g) grated mozzarella cheese

PIZZA DOUGH

2 teaspoons (7g) dried yeast
1 teaspoon sugar
¾ cup (180ml) warm water
2 cups (300g) plain flour
½ teaspoon salt

CARAMELISED ONIONS

1½ tablespoons light olive oil
16 baby (400g) onions, sliced
1 tablespoon sugar
1 tablespoon red wine vinegar

Grease 34cm pizza pan. Cut potatoes into 1cm cubes. Heat oil in pan, add potatoes, onion and garlic, cook, stirring, until onion is soft. Add stock, simmer, covered, over low heat about 30 minutes or until potatoes are very soft. Blend or process potato mixture until smooth; cool.

Spread potato mixture onto pizza dough, top evenly with caramelised onions and cheese. Bake in hot oven 25 minutes or until base is browned.

Pizza Dough: Combine yeast with sugar in small bowl, stir in water. Sift flour with salt in separate bowl, add yeast mixture, mix to a firm dough. Turn onto lightly floured surface, knead about 10 minutes or until smooth and elastic. Roll dough on lightly floured surface until large enough to fit prepared pan.

Caramelised Onions: Heat oil in pan, add onions, cook, stirring, until soft. Add sugar and vinegar, cook, stirring occasionally, until golden brown.

Serves 4.

- Recipe best made just before serving.
- Microwave: Not suitable.
- Freeze: Not suitable.

LEFT: From left: Garlic Potatoes with Couscous-Topped Chicken, Chicken, Pork and Potatoes in Peanut Sauce.
ABOVE: Potato Pizza with Caramelised Onions.

Left: Terracotta dish from Accoutrement. Above: China and cutlery from Ventura Design; cloth from Morris Home & Garden Wares.

Salads

Whether warm or cold, potatoes are a delicious contrast of texture, colour and flavour in these salads. Some are composed entirely of vegetables; others include heartier ingredients, such as smoked trout, mussels, tuna, beef, eggs, crisp bacon and chicken – all easy to put together. Tasty dressings, of course, are the perfect finishing touch.

WARM ENDIVE AND POTATO SALAD

30 baby (1.2kg) new potatoes
2 tablespoons olive oil
2 cloves garlic, crushed
1 medium bunch (150g) rocket
1 medium bunch (300g) curly endive
1 tablespoon balsamic vinegar
1 tablespoon seeded mustard
1 bunch (10) radishes, sliced
2 tablespoons chopped fresh chives

Cut potatoes into 5mm slices. Heat oil in pan, add garlic, cook potatoes in batches until brown and tender; drain on absorbent paper. Add rocket and endive to same pan, cook, stirring, until rocket and endive are just wilted. Add potatoes, vinegar and mustard, cook, stirring, until heated through. Stir in radishes and chives until just combined, serve immediately.

Serves 4 to 6.

■ Recipe best made close to serving.
■ Freeze: Not suitable.
■ Microwave: Not suitable.

KUMARA SALAD WITH PEPPERS AND HAM

2 medium (800g) kumara
1 medium (200g) yellow pepper
1 medium (200g) red pepper
200g sliced ham
2 tablespoons extra virgin olive oil
2 medium (300g) onions, sliced
2 cloves garlic, crushed

DRESSING
1/3 cup (80ml) extra virgin olive oil
1/3 cup (80ml) red wine vinegar
2 teaspoons brown sugar

Cut kumara into 1cm x 7cm strips, add to pan of boiling water, simmer, uncovered, about 4 minutes or until kumara is just tender, rinse under cold water; drain well.

Cut peppers and ham into thin strips. Heat oil in pan, add peppers, ham, onions and garlic, cook, stirring, until onions and peppers are very soft. Toss kumara gently with pepper mixture and dressing; serve warm or cold.

Dressing: Combine all ingredients in jar; shake well.

Serves 6.

■ Recipe can be made a day ahead.
■ Storage: Covered, in refrigerator.
■ Freeze: Not suitable.
■ Microwave: Kumara suitable.

RIGHT: From back: Warm Endive and Potato Salad, Kumara Salad with Peppers and Ham.

Mortar and pestle from Accoutrement; tea-towel from Home & Garden on the Mall.

CREAMY POTATO AND GHERKIN SALAD

5 large (1.5kg) potatoes
4 bacon rashers
6 hard-boiled eggs, quartered
2 sticks celery, sliced
6 green shallots, chopped
4 dill pickles, chopped
1/2 cup (125ml) mayonnaise
1/2 cup (125ml) sour cream
1/4 cup (60ml) milk

Peel potatoes, cut into large pieces. Boil, steam or microwave potatoes until tender; drain, cool. Cut bacon into strips, cook in dry pan until crisp; drain on absorbent paper. Combine potatoes, bacon, eggs, celery, shallots and pickles in large bowl; mix gently. Stir in combined mayonnaise, cream and milk.

Serves 6 to 8.

■ Recipe can be made several hours ahead.
■ Storage: Covered, in refrigerator.
■ Freeze: Not suitable.
■ Microwave: Potatoes suitable.

BACON AND BEAN SALAD WITH PEPPER DRESSING

1/2 cup (100g) dried haricot beans
4 medium (800g) potatoes, peeled, chopped
80g snow peas, halved
6 bacon rashers, chopped
1 medium cos lettuce
1/2 cup (40g) flaked parmesan cheese

DRESSING
3 medium (600g) red peppers
1/2 cup (125ml) light olive oil
1 tablespoon balsamic vinegar
1/2 teaspoon sugar

Place beans in bowl, cover well with cold water, cover; stand overnight.

Drain beans, add to pan of boiling water, simmer, uncovered, about 30 minutes or until beans are tender; drain, rinse under cold water; drain.

Boil, steam or microwave potatoes and snow peas separately until just tender; cool. Cook bacon in dry pan, stirring occasionally, until browned; drain on absorbent paper, cool.

Tear lettuce into medium-sized pieces, combine with beans, potatoes, snow peas and bacon in bowl; toss well. Drizzle salad with dressing, top with cheese.

Dressing: Quarter peppers, remove seeds and membranes. Grill peppers, skin side up, until skin blisters and blackens. Peel away skin, blend or process peppers until smooth. Combine peppers, oil, vinegar and sugar in jar; shake well.

Serves 4.

■ Recipe can be prepared a day ahead.
■ Storage: Covered, separately, in refrigerator.
■ Freeze: Beans suitable.
■ Microwave: Beans, potatoes and snow peas suitable.

POTATO BEAN SALAD WITH TANGY YOGURT DRESSING

2/3 cup (130g) dried haricot beans
18 baby (720g) new potatoes, halved
2 medium bunches (600g) curly endive
1 medium (150g) apple, thinly sliced
1 medium (250g) avocado, sliced
1/2 cup (50g) walnuts

DRESSING
1/2 cup (125ml) plain yogurt
1 egg yolk
1/2 cup (125ml) vegetable oil
1 tablespoon chopped fresh chives

Place beans in bowl, cover well with cold water, cover; stand overnight.

Drain beans, add to pan of boiling water, simmer, uncovered, about 30 minutes or until beans are tender; drain, rinse under cold water; drain.

Boil, steam or microwave potatoes until just tender; drain. Place endive leaves on plate, top with beans, potatoes, apple, avocado and nuts; drizzle with dressing.

Dressing: Process yogurt, egg yolk and oil until smooth, stir in chives.

Serves 6.

■ Beans can be cooked a day ahead.
■ Storage: Covered, in refrigerator.
■ Freeze: Beans suitable.
■ Microwave: Beans and potatoes suitable.

LEFT: From back: Bacon and Bean Salad with Pepper Dressing, Potato Bean Salad with Tangy Yogurt Dressing.
BELOW: Creamy Potato and Gherkin Salad.

Left: China from Villeroy & Boch; ladle from Morris Home & Garden Wares. Below: Pepper grinder and tea-towel from Accoutrement.

PEPPER AND POTATO SALAD WITH TUNA DRESSING

6 small (720g) potatoes
10 slices (100g) spicy salami
1 large green oak leaf lettuce
1 medium (200g) red pepper, sliced
½ cup (60g) seedless black olives

TUNA DRESSING
185g can tuna chunks in brine, drained
2 tablespoons chopped, drained capers
½ cup (125ml) mayonnaise
2 tablespoons lemon juice
1 tablespoon tomato paste
2 tablespoons chopped fresh basil
1 clove garlic, crushed

Boil, steam or microwave unpeeled potatoes until tender; drain, cool, slice. Cut salami slices into quarters. Combine potatoes, salami and torn lettuce leaves with remaining ingredients in serving bowl; drizzle with dressing.
Tuna Dressing: Blend or process all ingredients until smooth.

Serves 6.

■ Dressing best made just before serving.
■ Freeze: Not suitable.
■ Microwave: Potatoes suitable.

TRADITIONAL POTATO SALAD

5 medium (1kg) potatoes, peeled, chopped
5 green shallots, chopped
2 tablespoons chopped fresh parsley

MAYONNAISE
1 egg yolk
3 teaspoons lemon juice
1 clove garlic, crushed
½ teaspoon French mustard
¼ cup (60ml) olive oil
¼ cup (60ml) vegetable oil
1 tablespoon milk

Boil, steam or microwave potatoes until tender; cool. Combine potatoes, shallots, half the parsley and mayonnaise in bowl; mix well. Sprinkle with remaining parsley.

POTATO CAESAR SALAD

**4 small (480g) old potatoes, peeled
vegetable oil for deep-frying
1 tablespoon olive oil
3 bacon rashers, chopped
1 tablespoon chopped fresh thyme
1 medium cos lettuce
45g can anchovy fillets,
    drained, chopped
½ cup (40g) parmesan cheese flakes**

DRESSING
**1 egg
2 cloves garlic, crushed
1 teaspoon seeded mustard
½ teaspoon Worcestershire sauce
2 tablespoons lemon juice
¾ cup (180ml) olive oil**

Cut potatoes into 5mm cubes. Deep-fry potatoes in hot vegetable oil until browned and crisp; drain on absorbent paper.

Heat olive oil in pan, add bacon and thyme, cook, stirring, until bacon is browned and crisp. Combine most of the potatoes in bowl with torn lettuce leaves, anchovies, half the cheese, half the bacon and half the dressing; mix well. Drizzle with remaining dressing, sprinkle with remaining potatoes, cheese and bacon.

Dressing: Blend or process egg, garlic, mustard, sauce and juice until smooth. Add oil gradually in a thin stream while motor is operating.

Serves 4 to 6.

- Dressing can be made a day ahead.
- Storage: Covered, in refrigerator.
- Freeze: Not suitable.
- Microwave: Not suitable.

Mayonnaise: Blend or process egg yolk, juice, garlic and mustard until smooth. Add oils gradually in a thin stream while motor is operating, stir in milk.

Serves 4 to 6.

- Recipe can be made a day ahead.
- Storage: Covered, in refrigerator.
- Freeze: Not suitable.
- Microwave: Potatoes suitable.

ABOVE: From left: Pepper and Potato Salad with Tuna Dressing, Traditional Potato Salad. RIGHT: Potato Caesar Salad.

Above: Basket from Accoutrement; damask tablecloth from Lincraft. Right: Serving ware by Janine Schewkel at Mura Clay Gallery.

PEAR, POTATO AND BLUE VEIN CHEESE SALAD

30 baby (1.2kg) new potatoes, halved
15 (500g) baby pears, halved
160g snow pea sprouts
60g blue vein cheese, crumbled
¼ cup (40g) pine nuts, toasted

DRESSING
⅓ cup (80ml) light olive oil
2 tablespoons white wine vinegar
1 tablespoon honey
1 tablespoon chopped fresh chives
2 teaspoons lemon juice

Boil, steam or microwave potatoes until just tender; drain, cool. Combine potatoes and dressing in bowl, cover, refrigerate 1 hour; drain, reserve dressing. Combine potatoes and pears in bowl with sprouts and cheese; mix gently. Pour over reserved dressing, sprinkle with nuts.
Dressing: Combine all ingredients in jar; shake well.

Serves 4 to 6.

- Recipe can be prepared several hours ahead.
- Storage: Covered, in refrigerator.
- Freeze: Not suitable.
- Microwave: Potatoes suitable.

POTATO, PROSCIUTTO AND SUGAR SNAP PEA SALAD

300g sugar snap peas
4 medium (800g) potatoes
⅔ cup (160ml) olive oil
1 medium (170g) red Spanish onion, chopped
4 slices (40g) prosciutto, chopped
¼ cup (60ml) white wine vinegar
½ teaspoon coarsely ground black pepper
3 hard-boiled eggs, quartered
45g can flat anchovies, drained, halved
2 tablespoons chopped fresh chives
¼ cup (20g) parmesan cheese flakes

Add peas to pan of boiling water, return to boil; drain, rinse under cold water, drain. Boil, steam or microwave unpeeled potatoes until just tender; drain, cool 5 minutes, cut into 1.5cm slices.

Heat oil in pan, add onion, cook, uncovered, until soft. Add prosciutto, cook, stirring, 2 minutes; stir in vinegar and pepper. Combine peas, warm potatoes, half the eggs, anchovies, chives and onion mixture in large bowl; mix gently. Serve topped with remaining eggs and cheese.

Serves 6.

- Recipe best made close to serving.
- Freeze: Not suitable.
- Microwave: Peas and potatoes suitable.

NEW POTATO, BACON AND ARTICHOKE SALAD

10 baby (400g) new potatoes, quartered
1 bunch (650g) English spinach
6 bacon rashers, chopped
2 large (360g) carrots
280g Jerusalem artichokes
4 slices white bread

DRESSING
1 tablespoon tequila
1 tablespoon balsamic vinegar
1 tablespoon mild sweet chilli sauce
⅓ cup (80ml) olive oil
1 clove garlic, crushed

Boil, steam or microwave potatoes until tender; cool. Rinse spinach leaves thoroughly. Bring pan of water to boil, plunge leaves into boiling water; drain. Shred spinach coarsely; cool.

Cook bacon in dry pan until browned; drain on absorbent paper. Peel carrots and artichokes, cut into thin strips. Remove crusts from bread, flatten bread with rolling pin, cut into 5mm strips. Place strips onto lightly greased oven tray, toast in hot oven 5 minutes or until lightly browned and crisp.

Combine potatoes, spinach, bacon, carrots and artichokes in bowl with dressing, toss until well combined. Top salad with crisp bread strips.
Dressing: Combine all ingredients in jar; shake well.

Serves 4 to 6.

- Salad best made close to serving. Dressing can be made 3 days ahead.
- Storage: Dressing, covered, in refrigerator.
- Freeze: Not suitable.
- Microwave: Potatoes suitable.

LEFT: Pear, Potato and Blue Vein Cheese Salad.
RIGHT: From left: Potato, Prosciutto and Sugar Snap Pea Salad, New Potato, Bacon and Artichoke Salad.

Left: Cushion cover and salad servers from Morris Home & Garden Wares. Right: China from Kenwick Galleries.

CURRIED POTATO SALAD

38 baby (1.5kg) new potatoes, peeled
4 green shallots, chopped
¼ cup (40g) sultanas
1 tablespoon chopped fresh
  coriander
1 tablespoon chopped fresh mint
2 tablespoons pistachios, toasted

DRESSING
½ cup (125ml) mayonnaise
½ cup (125ml) sour cream
2 tablespoons fruit chutney
1 teaspoon bottled red curry paste
1 small clove garlic, crushed

Boil, steam or microwave potatoes until tender. Combine warm potatoes, shallots, sultanas, herbs and dressing in bowl; mix well. Sprinkle with nuts.

Dressing: Combine all ingredients in bowl; mix well.

Serves 6.

■ Recipe can be made 3 hours ahead.
■ Storage: Covered, in refrigerator.
■ Freeze: Not suitable.
■ Microwave: Potatoes suitable.

ABOVE: From left: Curried Potato Salad, Baked Kumara with Sesame Soy Dressing.
RIGHT: From left: Potato and Smoked Trout Salad, Potato and Mussel Salad.

Right: Jug from Accoutrement.

BAKED KUMARA WITH SESAME SOY DRESSING

2 large (1kg) kumara, peeled
2 tablespoons olive oil
1 large (200g) onion, sliced
2 cloves garlic, crushed
1 tablespoon chopped fresh thyme
2 green shallots, sliced
2 tablespoons sesame seeds, toasted

SESAME SOY DRESSING
3 teaspoons sesame oil
2 teaspoons soy sauce
2 tablespoons lemon juice
1 clove garlic, crushed

Cut kumara into 2cm pieces. Combine kumara, oil, onion, garlic and thyme in baking dish; mix well. Bake in moderate oven about 30 minutes or until kumara is tender; stir halfway through cooking; cool. Combine kumara mixture, shallots, seeds and dressing in bowl; mix well.
Sesame Soy Dressing: Combine all ingredients in small bowl; mix well.

Serves 4.

■ Recipe can be made a day ahead.
■ Storage: Covered, in refrigerator.
■ Freeze: Not suitable.
■ Microwave: Not suitable.

POTATO AND MUSSEL SALAD

1kg (36) small mussels
1 cup (250ml) dry white wine
1 cup (250ml) water
2 x 5cm strips lemon rind
1 medium (150g) onion, chopped
6 black peppercorns
25 baby (1kg) new potatoes, halved
30g butter
1 small (200g) leek, sliced
½ teaspoon fennel seeds, crushed

DRESSING
⅓ cup (80ml) mayonnaise
¼ cup (60ml) plain yogurt
1 teaspoon horseradish sauce
1 tablespoon chopped fresh dill

Scrub mussels, remove beards. Heat wine, water, rind, onion and peppercorns in large pan, add mussels, cook, covered, over high heat about 5 minutes or until mussels open. Drain mussels; discard liquid. Remove from shells, discard shells.

Boil, steam or microwave potatoes until tender. Heat butter in pan, add leek and seeds, cook, stirring, until leek is soft. Combine mussels, potatoes, leek mixture and dressing in bowl; mix well.
Dressing: Combine all ingredients in bowl; mix well.

Serves 4 to 6.

■ Recipe can be prepared 3 hours ahead.
■ Storage: Covered, in refrigerator.
■ Freeze: Not suitable.
■ Microwave: Potatoes suitable.

POTATO AND SMOKED TROUT SALAD

7 small (840g) potatoes, halved
250g whole smoked trout
½ small (50g) red Spanish onion, sliced
50g mixed salad leaves

DRESSING
⅓ cup (80ml) olive oil
1 tablespoon balsamic vinegar

Boil, steam or microwave potatoes until tender; drain. Remove skin from trout, remove bones; flake flesh into 1cm pieces. Combine potatoes, trout, onion, leaves and dressing in bowl; mix gently.
Dressing: Combine ingredients in jar; shake well.

Serves 4 to 6.

■ Recipe can be prepared several hours ahead.
■ Storage: Covered, separately, in refrigerator.
■ Freeze: Not suitable.
■ Microwave: Potatoes suitable.

SPICY POTATO SALAD

25 baby (1kg) new potatoes
1 teaspoon black mustard seeds
1 teaspoon ground cumin
1 teaspoon cumin seeds
1 clove garlic, crushed
2 tablespoons lemon juice
¼ cup chopped fresh coriander

Boil, steam or microwave potatoes until just tender, rinse under cold water; drain, cool. Heat dry pan, add spices, cook, stirring, until fragrant. Combine potatoes, spices and remaining ingredients in bowl; mix well.

Serves 6.

- Recipe can be made 3 hours ahead.
- Storage: Covered, in refrigerator.
- Freeze: Not suitable.
- Microwave: Potatoes suitable.

LAMB SALAD WITH STRAW POTATOES

Beef eye-fillet can be substituted for eye of lamb loin, if preferred.

2 medium (400g) old potatoes, peeled
vegetable oil for deep-frying
2 tablespoons olive oil
2 x 250g eye of lamb loins
2 tablespoons seeded mustard
150g mixed salad leaves

GARLIC MAYONNAISE
1 egg yolk
1 clove garlic, crushed
1 teaspoon balsamic vinegar
½ cup (125ml) vegetable oil
3 teaspoons warm water, approximately

Cut potatoes into 2mm slices. Cut slices lengthways into 2mm strips. Rinse potatoes under cold water until water runs clear, then soak in water for 1 hour. Drain potatoes well, pat dry with absorbent paper. Heat vegetable oil in large pan, deep-fry potatoes in batches until browned; drain on absorbent paper.

Heat olive oil in pan, add lamb, cook over high heat until browned all over. Spread lamb with mustard. Place lamb on wire rack in baking dish, bake in hot oven about 10 minutes or until cooked as desired. Stand 10 minutes before slicing.

Serve lamb on salad leaves with garlic mayonnaise and straw potatoes.
Garlic Mayonnaise: Combine egg yolk, garlic and vinegar in small bowl, gradually whisk in oil. Whisk in enough water to bring to desired consistency.

BEETROOT AND POTATO SALAD WITH FRESH DATES

5 medium (1kg) unpeeled potatoes, chopped
4 medium (640g) beetroot
2 sticks celery, sliced
4 green shallots, sliced
1 small (130g) green cucumber, sliced
4 seedless (80g) fresh dates, sliced

DRESSING
1 tablespoon chopped fresh coriander
2 tablespoons chopped fresh mint
2 tablespoons red wine vinegar
½ cup (125ml) olive oil

Boil, steam or microwave potatoes until just tender. Boil, steam or microwave un-peeled beetroot until tender; drain, cool. Peel beetroot, cut into wedges. Combine all ingredients in bowl; mix well. Pour over dressing; mix well.

Dressing: Combine all ingredients in jar; shake well.

Serves 6.

■ Salad can be partly made several hours ahead. Beetroot and dressing best stirred in just before serving.
■ Storage: Covered, in refrigerator.
■ Freeze: Not suitable.
■ Microwave: Potatoes and beetroot suitable.

Serves 6.
■ Mayonnaise can be prepared several hours ahead.
■ Storage: Covered, in refrigerator.
■ Freeze: Not suitable.
■ Microwave: Not suitable.

ABOVE: From left: Lamb Salad with Straw Potatoes, Spicy Potato Salad.
RIGHT: Beetroot and Potato Salad with Fresh Dates.

Above: Patterned plate from Villeroy & Boch; accessories from Morris Home & Garden Wares.
Right: Setting from Accoutrement.

GREEK POTATO SALAD

25 baby (1kg) new potatoes, halved
1 medium (200g) red pepper
1 medium (200g) yellow pepper
2 medium (260g) tomatoes, peeled
1 medium (170g) red Spanish
    onion, sliced
⅔ cup (100g) kalamata olives
200g feta cheese, cubed

DRESSING
⅓ cup (80ml) olive oil
1 tablespoon lemon juice
1 clove garlic, crushed
1 tablespoon chopped fresh dill
2 teaspoons chopped fresh thyme

Boil, steam or microwave potatoes until
tender; cool. Quarter peppers, remove
skin and membranes. Grill peppers, skin
side up, until skin blisters and blackens.
Peel away skin, slice peppers. Cut each
tomato into 8 wedges. Combine all ingredients in bowl; mix gently. Pour over
dressing; mix gently.
Dressing: Combine all ingredients in jar;
shake well.

Serves 6.

■ Recipe can be prepared a day ahead.
■ Storage: Covered, in refrigerator.
■ Freeze: Not suitable.
■ Microwave: Potatoes suitable.

CHICKEN, BEETROOT AND POTATO SALAD

4 medium (800g) potatoes, peeled
½ medium (230g) barbecued chicken
850g can whole baby beetroot,
    drained, halved
2 small (160g) onions, sliced
1 cup (50g) firmly packed
    watercress sprigs

DRESSING
½ cup (125ml) sour cream
1 tablespoon balsamic vinegar
1 tablespoon cream
1 tablespoon water
3 teaspoons sugar
1 teaspoon chopped fresh
    lemon thyme

Cut potatoes into 3cm pieces. Boil, steam
or microwave potatoes until just tender;
drain, rinse under cold water, drain.
Remove skin and bones from chicken;
slice chicken. Combine all ingredients in
bowl; mix gently. Place salad on serving
plate; drizzle with dressing.
Dressing: Combine all ingredients in
bowl; mix well.

Serves 4 to 6.

■ Recipe best made close to serving.
■ Freeze: Not suitable.
■ Microwave: Potatoes suitable.

WARM CRISPY POTATO SALAD

8 small (960g) potatoes
1 tablespoon olive oil
1 teaspoon fine sea salt
1 teaspoon seasoned pepper
1 tablespoon chopped fresh sage
4 bacon rashers, sliced
½ cup (55g) drained sun-dried tomatoes, sliced
¼ cup chopped fresh chives
1 coral lettuce
¼ cup (20g) parmesan cheese flakes

DRESSING
2 tablespoons olive oil
1 tablespoon red wine vinegar
1 clove garlic, crushed
1 teaspoon sugar

Cut each unpeeled potato into 6 wedges. Place potatoes in greased baking dish, toss potatoes in combined oil, salt and pepper, bake in moderately hot oven 30 minutes. Turn potatoes, sprinkle with sage, bake about further 30 minutes or until potatoes are crisp; keep warm.

Heat pan, add bacon, cook until crisp; drain on absorbent paper. Combine potatoes, bacon, tomatoes and chives in bowl, mix gently. Place lettuce leaves on serving plate, top with potato mixture, sprinkle with cheese flakes, drizzle with warm dressing.

Dressing: Combine all ingredients in pan; whisk over heat until warm.

Serves 4 to 6.

- Recipe best made close to serving.
- Freeze: Not suitable.
- Microwave: Not suitable.

LEFT: From back: Greek Potato Salad, Chicken, Beetroot and Potato Salad.
BELOW: Warm Crispy Potato Salad.

Left: China from Villeroy & Boch; spoon and metal bowl from Morris Home & Garden Wares.
Below: Spoon from Morris Home & Garden Wares.

MARINATED BEEF AND POTATO SALAD

500g beef eye-fillet
1 tablespoon walnut oil
1 tablespoon honey
¼ cup (60ml) red wine vinegar
1 teaspoon ground fennel
pinch cayenne pepper
1 tablespoon olive oil
18 baby (720g) new potatoes, halved
250g cherry tomatoes
100g snow peas, halved
160g snow pea sprouts

DRESSING
⅓ cup (80ml) extra light olive oil
2 teaspoons red wine vinegar
2 tablespoons seeded mustard
1 teaspoon mild sweet chilli sauce
1 teaspoon honey

Cut beef into thin strips. Combine beef, walnut oil, honey, vinegar, fennel and pepper in bowl; cover, refrigerate overnight.

Heat olive oil in pan, cook beef in batches over high heat until browned and tender. Boil, steam or microwave potatoes until tender; cool. Combine beef, potatoes, tomatoes and snow peas in bowl; mix well. Place snow pea sprouts in serving dish, top with beef mixture, drizzle with dressing.

Dressing: Combine all ingredients in jar; shake well.

Serves 6 to 8.

- ■ Recipe can be prepared a day ahead.
- ■ Storage: Covered, separately, in refrigerator.
- ■ Freeze: Not suitable.
- ■ Microwave: Potatoes suitable.

ITALIAN POTATO SALAD

25 baby (1kg) new potatoes, halved
150g green beans
250g cherry tomatoes, halved

DRESSING
2 tablespoons red wine vinegar
1 tablespoon olive oil
1 tablespoon chopped fresh thyme

Boil, steam or microwave potatoes until tender, rinse under cold water; drain. Place warm potatoes in bowl, add dressing, mix gently; cool. Cut beans into 4cm lengths. Boil, steam or microwave beans until tender, rinse under cold water; drain, cool. Combine potato mixture, beans and tomatoes; mix gently.

Dressing: Combine all ingredients in jar; shake well.

Serves 6.

- ■ Recipe can be prepared several hours ahead.
- ■ Storage: Covered, separately, in refrigerator.
- ■ Freeze: Not suitable.
- ■ Microwave: Potatoes and beans suitable.

OYSTER MUSHROOM AND POTATO SALAD

15 baby (600g) new potatoes, halved
1 medium (250g) avocado
1 tablespoon Dijon mustard
1 clove garlic, crushed
1 egg
2 tablespoons lemon juice
½ cup (125ml) olive oil
⅓ cup (80ml) water
¼ cup chopped fresh chives
300g oyster mushrooms
250g cherry tomatoes

Boil, steam or microwave potatoes until tender; cool. Blend or process avocado, mustard, garlic, egg and juice until just combined. Add oil gradually in a thin stream while motor is operating. Stir in water and chives. Combine potatoes, avocado mixture, mushrooms and tomatoes in large bowl, mix well.

Serves 4.

- ■ Recipe can be prepared a day ahead.
- ■ Storage: Separately, covered, in refrigerator.
- ■ Freeze: Not suitable.
- ■ Microwave: Potatoes suitable.

LEFT: From back: Marinated Beef and Potato Salad, Italian Potato Salad.
BELOW: Oyster Mushroom and Potato Salad.

Accompaniments

All of these recipes are designed to be accompaniments, but many could easily be a light meal. They are so tasty — some creamy, some crispy, some spiced, some saucy, with lots of fresh flavour combinations to discover and enjoy. We also give our favourite recipes for traditional roast and mashed potatoes (we're often asked for these), plus the secret of making our best ever chips.

POTATO RATATOUILLE

1 tablespoon olive oil
1 medium (150g) onion, chopped
2 cloves garlic, crushed
12 baby (480g) new potatoes, halved
425g can tomatoes
1 teaspoon sugar
1 tablespoon tomato paste
1 small (150g) red pepper, chopped
1 small (150g) green pepper, chopped
2 teaspoons chopped fresh thyme
2 teaspoons chopped fresh oregano
2 medium (240g) zucchini, sliced

Heat oil in pan, add onion, garlic and potatoes, cook, stirring, 5 minutes or until potatoes are lightly browned. Add undrained crushed tomatoes, sugar, paste, peppers and herbs, cook, covered, 20 minutes. Add zucchini, cook, covered, 10 minutes or until all vegetables are tender.
Serves 4.

▓ Recipe can be made a day ahead.
▓ Storage: Covered, in refrigerator.
▓ Freeze: Not suitable.
▓ Microwave: Suitable.

POTATO RICE BAKE

You will need to cook about ⅓ cup (65g) long-grain rice for this recipe.

5 medium (1kg) old potatoes, peeled, thinly sliced
1 cup cooked long-grain rice
50g butter, chopped
1½ cups (185g) grated gruyere cheese
1½ cups (185g) grated tasty cheddar cheese
50g butter, melted, extra
1 teaspoon Szechwan pepper

Grease shallow ovenproof dish (2 litre/8 cup capacity). Place one-third of the potatoes over base of prepared dish, top with half of the rice and butter and a third of the cheeses. Repeat layering with more potatoes, rice, butter and another third of the cheeses; top with remaining potatoes. Press down lightly, pour over combined extra butter and pepper, sprinkle with remaining cheeses. Bake, uncovered, in moderately hot oven about 1 hour or until potatoes are tender and top is browned.

Serves 4 to 6.
▓ Recipe can be made 3 hours ahead.
▓ Storage: Covered, in refrigerator.
▓ Freeze: Not suitable.
▓ Microwave: Not suitable.

RIGHT: From back: Potato Ratatouille, Potato Rice Bake.

BABY NEW POTATOES WITH FOUR TOPPINGS

18 baby (720g) new potatoes

TOMATO
1 tablespoon olive oil
2 cloves garlic, crushed
1 small (200g) leek, chopped
425g can tomatoes
1 tablespoon tomato paste
1 teaspoon sugar
1 tablespoon chopped fresh oregano
2 tablespoons chopped fresh basil

YOGURT HERB
½ cup (125ml) plain yogurt
⅓ cup (80ml) sour cream
¼ cup chopped fresh chives
2 tablespoons chopped fresh coriander
2 teaspoons mild sweet chilli sauce

MUSHROOM
30g butter
3 green shallots, chopped
200g button mushrooms, sliced
½ small (75g) red pepper, chopped
½ cup (125ml) cream
½ teaspoon chicken stock powder
2 teaspoons chopped fresh thyme
1 tablespoon chopped fresh rosemary

PESTO
1 cup firmly packed fresh basil leaves
¼ cup (40g) pine nuts, toasted
1 clove garlic, crushed
2 tablespoons olive oil
¼ cup (20g) grated parmesan cheese
⅓ cup (80ml) cream
1 tablespoon water

Boil, steam or microwave potatoes until tender. Serve potatoes with any of the following toppings.

Tomato: Heat oil in pan, add garlic and leek, cook, stirring, until leek is soft. Add undrained crushed tomatoes, paste and sugar, simmer, uncovered, about 5 minutes or until thickened slightly. Stir in herbs.

Yogurt Herb: Combine all ingredients in bowl; mix well.

Mushroom: Heat butter in pan, add shallots, mushrooms and pepper, cook, stirring, until shallots and mushrooms are soft. Add cream and stock powder, simmer, stirring, about 5 minutes or until slightly thickened. Stir in herbs.

Pesto: Process basil, nuts and garlic until finely chopped. Add oil in a thin stream while motor is operating, process until

TRADITIONAL ROAST POTATOES

5 medium (1kg) potatoes, peeled
2 tablespoons olive oil
40g butter, melted
1 teaspoon salt

Cut potatoes into uniform sizes. Cook potatoes in pan of boiling water 5 minutes. Drain, cool on absorbent paper. Combine potatoes, oil and butter in baking dish; mix well. Sprinkle with salt; bake in hot oven for about 1 hour or until tender.

Serves 4.

■ Potatoes best cooked just before serving.
■ Freeze: Not suitable.
■ Microwave: Partly cooked potatoes suitable.

LEFT: Baby New Potatoes with Four Toppings: clockwise from right: Yogurt Herb, Pesto, Tomato, and Mushroom.
BELOW: Traditional Roast Potatoes.

Left: Setting from Grace Bros.

combined. Add cheese, process until combined. Stir in cream and water.

Each topping serves 4.

■ Toppings can be made a day ahead.
■ Storage: Covered, separately, in refrigerator.
■ Freeze: Not suitable.
■ Microwave: Potatoes suitable.

BUBBLE AND SQUEAK

Leftover baked or boiled vegetables can be used in this recipe, if desired.

4 medium (800g) old potatoes, peeled
2 medium (240g) carrots
250g peeled pumpkin
1 large (200g) onion, chopped
1 cup (125g) frozen peas
1 cup (80g) shredded cabbage
30g butter
2 tablespoons vegetable oil

Boil, steam or microwave potatoes until tender; drain, mash, cool. Cut carrots and pumpkin into 2cm pieces. Cook carrots, pumpkin, onion, peas and cabbage separately in pan of boiling water until tender; drain. Combine mashed potato with all vegetables in bowl; mix well.

Heat butter and oil in 32cm frying pan; add vegetable mixture, press down with eggslice, cook, without stirring, until browned underneath. Cut into serving pieces, using eggslice, turn pieces over, cook until browned on other side.

Serves 6.

- Recipe can be made a day ahead.
- Storage: Covered, in refrigerator.
- Freeze: Not suitable.
- Microwave: Vegetables suitable.

BELOW: Bubble and Squeak.
RIGHT: From left: Saute Artichoke Hearts and Potatoes, Kumara with Pear and Currants.

SAUTE ARTICHOKE HEARTS AND POTATOES

25 baby (1kg) new potatoes, peeled, halved
2 x 280g jars artichoke hearts in olive oil
1 small (80g) onion, finely chopped
2 cloves garlic, crushed
1 tablespoon chopped fresh thyme

Boil, steam or microwave potatoes until tender; drain, pat dry with absorbent paper. Drain artichoke hearts, reserve ¼ cup (60ml) of the oil; cut artichokes in half. Heat reserved oil in pan, add onion, garlic and thyme, cook, stirring occasionally, until onion is soft. Add potatoes and artichokes, cook, stirring occasionally,

until vegetables are heated through and potatoes are lightly browned.

Serves 4 to 6.

- Recipe best made close to serving.
- Freeze: Not suitable.
- Microwave: Potatoes suitable.

KUMARA WITH PEAR AND CURRANTS

3 medium (1.2kg) kumara, peeled, chopped
60g butter
1 medium (150g) onion, finely chopped
1 teaspoon grated orange rind
¼ cup (60ml) orange juice
¾ cup (180ml) chicken stock
6 dried juniper berries
1 teaspoon ground cinnamon
1 large (330g) pear, peeled, cored, chopped
¼ cup (35g) dried currants
1 tablespoon honey
2 tablespoons chopped fresh parsley
2 tablespoons chopped roasted pecans

Boil, steam or microwave kumara until just tender; drain, rinse under cold water, drain. Heat butter in pan, add onion, rind and juice, cook, stirring, until onion is soft. Add stock, berries, cinnamon, pear, currants and honey, cook, stirring, about 8 minutes or until pear is tender. Gently stir kumara into onion mixture, stir until heated through. Serve sprinkled with parsley and nuts.

Serves 6.

- Recipe can be made 3 hours ahead.
- Storage: Covered, in refrigerator.
- Freeze: Not suitable.
- Microwave: Kumara suitable.

77

NEW POTATOES COOKED IN MILK

5 medium (1kg) new potatoes, peeled, sliced
1 litre (4 cups) milk

TOPPING
3 bacon rashers, chopped
2 tablespoons chopped fresh basil
¼ cup (20g) grated parmesan cheese
2 teaspoons chopped fresh thyme
1 clove garlic, crushed

Place potatoes in large pan, cover with milk, slowly simmer, uncovered, skimming top when necessary, until potatoes are tender; drain, discard milk.

Layer potatoes in ovenproof dish (1.75 litre/ 7 cup capacity), sprinkle with topping. Cook, uncovered, in hot oven 15 minutes or until potatoes are heated through.
Topping: Add bacon to dry pan, cook, stirring, until crisp; cool. Combine bacon, basil, cheese, thyme and garlic in bowl; mix well.

Serves 4 to 6.

- Recipe best made close to serving.
- Freeze: Not suitable.
- Microwave: Bacon and potatoes suitable.

ROAST POTATOES WITH PARSNIPS AND BACON ROLLS

8 small (960g) old potatoes, peeled
¼ cup (60ml) olive oil
30g butter, melted
3 medium (375g) parsnips, halved
2 large (400g) onions, quartered
6 bacon rashers
2 teaspoons chopped fresh sage

Boil potatoes 10 minutes; drain. Combine oil, butter, potatoes, parsnips and onions in large baking dish; mix well. Bake in very hot oven 30 minutes. Cut each bacon rasher in half, lengthways, roll up and secure with toothpicks. Add to potato mixture, bake further 15 minutes or until bacon is crisp. Remove toothpicks, sprinkle with sage.

Serves 6.

- Recipe best made just before serving.
- Freeze: Not suitable.
- Microwave: Not suitable.

SAUTE POTATOES PROVENCALE

25 baby (1kg) new potatoes, halved
⅓ cup (80ml) virgin olive oil
1 large (300g) red Spanish onion, sliced
1 small (150g) red pepper, sliced
2 medium (240g) zucchini, sliced
2 teaspoons fresh rosemary leaves
¼ cup (60ml) lemon juice
2 cloves garlic, crushed
1 tablespoon shredded fresh basil leaves

Boil, steam or microwave potatoes until almost tender; drain. Heat oil in large pan, add onion, pepper, zucchini and rosemary; cook, stirring, until onion is soft. Add potatoes, cook about 10 minutes or until potatoes are lightly browned. Pour over lemon juice, add garlic and basil; mix well.

Serves 6.

- Recipe best made close to serving.
- Freeze: Not suitable.
- Microwave: Potatoes suitable.

LEFT: From back: New Potatoes Cooked in Milk, Roast Potatoes with Parsnips and Bacon Rolls.
RIGHT: Saute Potatoes Provencale.

Left: Ovenware from Accoutrement. Right: Basket and plant pots from Barbara's Storehouse.

QUARTET OF BUTTERS FOR POTATOES

5 medium (1kg) potatoes, chopped

SALAMI CHEESE
125g soft butter
50g mild salami, finely chopped
¼ cup (20g) grated parmesan cheese
1 teaspoon seasoned pepper

TOMATO OLIVE
125g soft butter
**⅓ cup (45g) drained chopped
    sun-dried tomatoes**
**2 tablespoons chopped seedless
    black olives**
2 teaspoons chopped fresh basil

HAZELNUT ORANGE
125g soft butter
**2 tablespoons hazelnuts, roasted,
    chopped**
½ teaspoon grated orange rind
2 teaspoons orange juice

THAI-STYLE
125g soft butter
**1 tablespoon chopped fresh
    coriander**
1 tablespoon chopped fresh mint
2 teaspoons lime juice
**1 small fresh red chilli, seeded,
    finely chopped**

Boil, steam or microwave potatoes until
tender; drain. Serve potatoes with any of
the butters.
For each butter: Combine all ingredients
in bowl; mix well. Spoon onto sheet of foil,
shape into 18cm log, roll up firmly, twisting
ends of foil. Refrigerate until firm. Or,
serve butters in bowls, if desired.

Each butter serves 6.

- ■ Butters can be made 2 days ahead.
- ■ Storage: Covered, in refrigerator.
- ■ Freeze: Suitable.
- ■ Microwave: Potatoes suitable.

*RIGHT: Centre: Tomato Olive Butter. Small
bowls from left: Hazelnut Orange Butter,
Thai-Style Butter, Salami Cheese Butter.*

POTATOES AND ONIONS WITH WALNUTS

2 tablespoons walnut oil
⅓ cup (80ml) olive oil
2 large (400g) onions, sliced
3 large (900g) new potatoes, sliced
¾ cup (75g) walnuts
1 tablespoon chopped fresh oregano

Heat half the oils in baking dish, add onions, cook, stirring, until onions are well browned; remove from dish. Heat remaining oils in same dish, add potatoes, cook, stirring, until potatoes are well browned all over. Add nuts and onions; mix gently. Bake in hot oven about 15 minutes or until heated through. Sprinkle with oregano.

Serves 4.

■ Recipe best made just before serving.
■ Freeze: Not suitable.
■ Microwave: Not suitable.

CARAWAY POTATOES AND SWEDES IN CREAM

Do not use thickened cream.

2 medium (450g) swedes, peeled
1 teaspoon caraway seeds
4 medium (800g) old potatoes, peeled, thinly sliced
¾ cup (90g) grated tasty cheddar cheese
1 cup (250ml) cream

Grease ovenproof dish (2 litre/8 cup capacity). Cut swedes into thin strips. Place swedes in prepared dish, sprinkle with seeds, top with potatoes, sprinkle with cheese. Carefully pour cream over cheese. Cover dish with foil, bake in moderate oven 45 minutes; remove foil, bake further 45 minutes or until potatoes are tender and browned.

Serves 6.

■ Recipe best made just before serving.
■ Freeze: Not suitable.
■ Microwave: Suitable.

BRAISED CELERY AND POTATOES

30g butter
6 baby (150g) onions, peeled
1 stick celery, sliced
5 medium (1kg) potatoes, peeled, sliced
¼ cup (60ml) dry white wine
¾ cup (180ml) chicken stock
1 tablespoon chopped fresh dill

Melt butter in large pan, add onions, celery and potatoes, cook until celery is softened slightly. Add wine and stock, simmer, covered, about 20 minutes or until potatoes are tender. Stir in dill.

Serves 4 to 6.

■ Recipe can be made 3 hours ahead.
■ Storage: Covered, in refrigerator.
■ Freeze: Not suitable.
■ Microwave: Suitable.

POTATOES AND MUSHROOMS BAKED IN CREAM

Do not use thickened cream.

80g butter
1 tablespoon vegetable oil
400g button mushrooms, sliced
2 cloves garlic, crushed
1 cup (250ml) cream
2 green shallots, chopped
1 tablespoon chopped fresh thyme
¼ cup (20g) grated parmesan cheese
5 medium (1kg) old potatoes, peeled, thinly sliced
½ cup (75g) plain flour, approximately

TOPPING
½ cup (60g) grated tasty cheddar cheese
¼ cup (20g) grated parmesan cheese
2 tablespoons chopped fresh chives
1 tablespoon chopped fresh thyme

Heat butter and oil in large frying pan, add mushrooms and garlic, cook, stirring, about 8 minutes or until mushrooms are tender and liquid has evaporated; drain on absorbent paper. Combine mushroom mixture, cream, shallots, thyme and cheese in bowl; mix well.

Grease shallow ovenproof dish (1.75 litre/7 cup capacity). Toss potatoes in flour, shake away excess flour. Layer potatoes in prepared dish, pour over mushroom mixture, sprinkle with topping. Bake, uncovered, in moderate oven about 1 hour or until potatoes are tender.

Topping: Combine all ingredients in small bowl; mix well.

Serves 4 to 6.

■ Recipe can be prepared several hours ahead.
■ Storage: Covered, in refrigerator.
■ Freeze: Not suitable.
■ Microwave: Not suitable.

LEFT: From left: Caraway Potatoes and Swedes in Cream, Potatoes and Onions with Walnuts.
BELOW: From left: Potatoes and Mushrooms Baked in Cream, Braised Celery and Potatoes.

PARSNIP AND POTATO PUREE

2 medium (250g) parsnips,
    peeled, chopped
2 medium (400g) potatoes, peeled,
    chopped
2 tablespoons cream
20g butter
2 teaspoons chopped fresh thyme

Boil, steam or microwave parsnips and potatoes separately until tender. Process parsnips until smooth. Mash potatoes with cream and butter until almost smooth. Add to parsnip puree in processor, process until just combined. Stir in thyme.

Serves 4.

- Recipe best made close to serving.
- Freeze: Not suitable.
- Microwave: Suitable.

MIXED VEGETABLE PUREE

1 medium (300g) eggplant
2 tablespoons olive oil
1 medium (150g) onion, chopped
1 clove garlic, crushed
1 teaspoon ground cumin
½ teaspoon ground coriander
1 medium (400g) kumara,
    peeled, chopped
1 large (300g) potato,
    peeled, chopped
1 large (180g) carrot, chopped
¾ cup (180ml) chicken stock
1 small red chilli, seeded,
    finely chopped
1 tablespoon chopped fresh
    coriander

Place whole eggplant on oven tray, bake, uncovered, in hot oven about 1 hour or until soft; cool 10 minutes. Peel and chop eggplant. Heat oil in pan, add onion, garlic, cumin and ground coriander, cook, stirring, until onion is soft. Add kumara, potato, carrot and stock, simmer, covered, about 30 minutes or until vegetables are soft.

Blend or process eggplant, potato mixture, chilli and fresh coriander until smooth.

Serves 4.

- Recipe can be made a day ahead.
- Storage: Covered, in refrigerator.
- Freeze: Not suitable.
- Microwave: Not suitable.

CHILLI, PEPPER AND POTATO PUREE

3 large (900g) old potatoes,
    peeled, chopped
2 cups (500ml) fish stock
2 cloves garlic, crushed
2 small fresh red chillies, chopped
¼ teaspoon ground turmeric
1 medium (200g) red pepper
¼ cup (60ml) olive oil

Add potatoes to pan with stock, garlic, chillies and turmeric, boil until potatoes are tender; drain, reserve ⅓ cup (80ml) of stock. Quarter pepper, remove seeds and membranes. Grill pepper, skin side up, until skin blisters and blackens. Peel skin away, chop pepper.

Mash potatoes, push through a fine sieve, stir in pepper. Gradually add oil in a thin stream, stirring constantly. Gradually add reserved stock to form a soft paste.

Serves 6.

- Recipe best made close to serving.
- Freeze: Not suitable.
- Microwave: Potatoes suitable.

POTATOES A LA DAUPHINOISE

Do not use thickened cream.

4 large (1.2kg) old potatoes, peeled,
    thinly sliced
pinch ground nutmeg
300ml cream
¼ cup (20g) grated parmesan cheese
20g butter, chopped

Grease deep 19cm square cake pan. Layer potatoes in prepared pan, sprinkle with nutmeg. Pour over cream, sprinkle with cheese, dot with butter. Cover, bake in moderate oven 30 minutes, uncover, continue baking about 45 minutes or until top is browned and potatoes are tender.

Serves 4 to 6.

- Recipe can be made a day ahead.
- Storage: Covered, in refrigerator.
- Freeze: Not suitable.
- Microwave: Not suitable.

LEFT: Clockwise from left: Parsnip and Potato Puree, Mixed Vegetable Puree, Chilli, Pepper and Potato Puree. RIGHT: Potatoes a la Dauphinoise.

Left: Tiles from Perfect Ceramics; box from Barbara's Storehouse. Right: Plate from Basic Essentials.

BEST EVER CHIPS

Oil should be heated to 180°C for the first frying of chips; 200°C for the second frying.

4 large (1.2kg) old potatoes, peeled
vegetable oil for deep-frying

Cut potatoes into 8mm slices, then into 8mm strips or finer, if you prefer. Place chips in large bowl, cover with water, stand 30 minutes; drain.

Dry chips thoroughly with clean tea-towel before frying. Heat enough oil in deep frying pan to come halfway up side of pan. Add chips gradually in batches, so oil will not spatter. Cook for a few minutes or until chips barely change colour; drain well on absorbent paper. Reheat oil, fry chips again in batches until lightly browned. Drain well on absorbent paper, serve immediately.

Serves 4 to 6.

■ Recipe best made just before serving.
■ Freeze: Not suitable.
■ Microwave: Not suitable.

CHILLI POTATO PATTIES

2 large (600g) old potatoes,
  peeled, chopped
1 tablespoon vegetable oil
1 small (80g) onion, finely chopped
1 (20g) bottled jalapeno pepper,
  seeded, finely chopped
1 egg, separated
⅔ cup (80g) grated tasty
  cheddar cheese
¾ cup (120g) cornmeal
⅓ cup (80ml) water
⅓ cup (50g) plain flour
⅓ cup (55g) cornmeal, extra
vegetable oil for shallow-frying

Boil, steam or microwave potatoes until tender; drain, mash well, cool 10 minutes. Heat oil in pan, add onion and pepper, cook, stirring, until onion is soft; cool. Combine potato, onion mixture, egg yolk, cheese and cornmeal in bowl; mix well. Gradually stir in water.

Divide mixture into 8 portions, shape into patties, toss in flour, shake away excess flour. Dip patties in lightly beaten egg white, roll in extra cornmeal, refrigerate 30 minutes. Heat oil in pan, add patties in batches, shallow-fry until golden brown on both sides; drain on absorbent paper.

Makes 8.

■ Recipe can be made a day ahead.
■ Storage: Covered, in refrigerator.
■ Freeze: Suitable.
■ Microwave: Potatoes suitable.

GRILLED POTATOES WITH GARLIC

5 medium (1kg) old potatoes, peeled
¼ cup (60ml) olive oil
2 cloves garlic, crushed
1 tablespoon chopped fresh rosemary
1 tablespoon chopped fresh parsley
1 teaspoon seeded mustard
2 teaspoons lemon juice
30g butter, melted

Cut potatoes into large wedges. Place onto greased oven trays, bake in moderately hot oven about 30 minutes or until just tender; cool.

Combine oil, garlic, herbs, mustard and juice in bowl, add potatoes, toss until potatoes are well coated with mixture. Return potatoes to oven trays, brush with butter, cook under hot grill until golden brown, turning potatoes when necessary. Serve sprinkled with salt, if desired.

Serves 4.

■ Recipe best made just before serving.
■ Freeze: Not suitable.
■ Microwave: Not suitable.

LEFT: Best Ever Chips.
RIGHT: From back: Chilli Potato Patties, Grilled Potatoes with Garlic.

Right: Serviette from Barbara's Storehouse.

CORIANDER POTATOES WITH CHICKPEAS AND TOMATOES

2 tablespoons olive oil
1 large (200g) onion, sliced
2 cloves garlic, crushed
2 teaspoons ground cumin
2 teaspoons ground coriander
4 medium (800g) old potatoes, peeled, sliced
425g can tomatoes
1 tablespoon tomato paste
1 teaspoon sugar
1¼ cups (310ml) water
310g can chickpeas, rinsed, drained
¼ cup chopped fresh coriander

Heat oil in pan, add onion and garlic, cook, stirring, until onion is soft. Add cumin and coriander, cook, stirring, 3 minutes or until fragrant. Add potatoes, cook, stirring, until potatoes are lightly browned.

Stir in undrained crushed tomatoes, paste, sugar and water, simmer, covered, 25 minutes or until potatoes are tender. Add chickpeas and coriander, cook, stirring, until heated through.

Serves 4.

- Recipe can be made a day ahead.
- Storage: Covered, in refrigerator.
- Freeze: Not suitable.
- Microwave: Not suitable.

GRATIN OF FENNEL AND POTATO

Do not use thickened cream.

2 tablespoons olive oil
1 medium (350g) leek, sliced
1 small (450g) fennel bulb, thinly sliced
2 cloves garlic, crushed
2 medium (400g) old potatoes, peeled, thinly sliced
1 cup (250ml) cream

TOPPING
1 cup (70g) stale breadcrumbs
½ cup (40g) grated parmesan cheese
30g butter, melted

Heat oil in pan, add leek, fennel and garlic, cook, stirring, until leek and fennel are soft. Place potatoes over base of shallow ovenproof dish (1.5 litre/6 cup capacity), top with leek and fennel mixture, pour over cream.

Sprinkle topping over cream, bake, uncovered, in moderate oven about 1 hour or until topping is browned and potatoes are tender.
Topping: Combine all ingredients in bowl; mix well.

Serves 6.

- Recipe can be made a day ahead.
- Storage: Covered, in refrigerator.
- Freeze: Not suitable.
- Microwave: Leek and fennel mixture suitable.

MUSTARD POTATOES WITH SPINACH

30g butter
1 medium (150g) onion, finely chopped
25 baby (1kg) new potatoes, halved
1 clove garlic, crushed
1 cup (250ml) chicken stock
2 teaspoons seeded mustard
1 tablespoon cream
½ bunch (325g) English spinach, roughly chopped

Heat butter in large pan, add onion, cook, stirring, until onion is soft. Add potatoes, garlic, stock and mustard, simmer, covered, about 20 minutes or until potatoes are tender. Add cream and spinach, simmer, covered, until spinach is just wilted.

Serves 4 to 6.

- Recipe can be made 3 hours ahead.
- Storage: Covered, in refrigerator.
- Freeze: Not suitable.
- Microwave: Suitable.

POTATO AND RICOTTA STRUDEL

Strudel filling has a slightly grainy texture.

40g butter
1 medium (350g) leek, sliced
3 bacon rashers, finely chopped
1 clove garlic, crushed
2 medium (400g) old potatoes, peeled, chopped
500g ricotta cheese
½ cup (40g) grated parmesan cheese
1 egg, lightly beaten
pinch ground nutmeg
2 teaspoons chopped fresh thyme
2 tablespoons chopped fresh chives
8 sheets fillo pastry
60g butter, melted, extra

TOPPING
½ cup (60g) grated tasty cheddar cheese
¼ cup (15g) stale breadcrumbs

Heat butter in pan, add leek, bacon and garlic, cook, stirring, until leek is soft. Boil, steam or microwave potatoes until tender; drain. Push potato and ricotta through fine sieve. Combine potato and ricotta with leek mixture, parmesan cheese, egg, nutmeg and herbs; mix well.

Layer pastry sheets together, brushing each with some of the extra butter. Shape potato mixture into 10cm x 30cm rectangle along centre of pastry. Fold in ends, roll over to enclose filling. Place strudel seam side down on oven tray, brush with extra butter, sprinkle with topping. Bake in moderately hot oven 25 minutes, reduce heat to moderate, bake further 15 minutes or until browned.

Topping: Combine both ingredients in bowl; mix well.

Serves 6.

- Recipe best made just before serving, although filling can be made a day ahead.
- Storage: Covered, in refrigerator.
- Freeze: Not suitable.
- Microwave: Potatoes suitable.

LEFT: From back: Gratin of Fennel and Potato, Coriander Potatoes with Chickpeas and Tomatoes.
RIGHT: From back: Potato and Ricotta Strudel, Mustard Potatoes with Spinach.

Right: Bowl and plate from The Bay Tree Kitchen Shop.

POTATOES ANNA

**4 large (1.2kg) yellow-fleshed
  potatoes, peeled
100g butter, melted
salt, pepper**

Cut potatoes into very thin slices, pat dry with absorbent paper. Brush butter generously over 23cm round enamel-coated cast iron pan with sloping sides, or ovenproof pie plate. Place a layer of over-lapping potato slices over base of prepared pan, brush with butter, sprinkle with salt and pepper. Repeat layering until all slices are used, ending with butter.

Cover with foil, bake in hottest part of very hot oven 20 minutes. Remove foil, bake further 30 minutes or until top is crisp and golden brown and potatoes are cooked through. Turn onto plate, cut into wedges to serve.

Serves 6.

- Recipe best made close to serving.
- Freeze: Not suitable.
- Microwave: Not suitable.

POTATO, ONION AND ANCHOVY BAKE

Do not use thickened cream.

**5 medium (1kg) old potatoes, peeled,
  thinly sliced
2 cloves garlic, peeled
pinch ground nutmeg
300ml cream
1 small (80g) onion, sliced
6 anchovy fillets, drained, chopped
½ cup (40g) grated parmesan cheese
½ cup (60g) grated tasty cheddar cheese
2 tablespoons pine nuts**

Grease 17cm x 23cm ovenproof dish (1.25 litre/5 cup capacity). Combine potatoes, garlic, nutmeg and cream in pan; simmer 5 minutes. Drain, reserve cream, discard garlic. Layer potatoes, onion and anchovies in prepared dish, pour over reserved cream; top with cheeses and sprinkle with pine nuts. Bake, uncovered, in moderate oven about 45 minutes or until potatoes are tender.

Serves 4 to 6.

- Recipe can be prepared 3 hours ahead.
- Storage: Covered, in refrigerator.
- Freeze: Not suitable.
- Microwave: Not suitable.

*BELOW: From back: Potato, Onion and Anchovy Bake, Potato and Kumara Gratin.
BELOW LEFT: Potatoes Anna.*

*Below: Tea-towel from Barbara's Storehouse.
Below left: Serviette from Barbara's Storehouse.*

POTATO AND KUMARA GRATIN

6 small (720g) potatoes, peeled
2 small (500g) kumara, peeled
60g butter
¼ cup (35g) plain flour
1¼ cups (310ml) milk
½ cup (125ml) chicken stock
⅓ cup (40g) grated Swiss cheese
2 teaspoons French mustard
¼ cup (30g) grated Swiss cheese, extra
2 tablespoons flaked almonds
¼ teaspoon paprika

Grease 4 shallow ovenproof dishes (1⅓ cup/330ml capacity). Cut potatoes and kumara into 5mm slices. Boil, steam or microwave potatoes and kumara separately until just tender; drain, cool.

Heat butter in pan, add flour, stir over heat until bubbly. Remove from heat, gradually stir in milk and stock, return to heat, stir until sauce boils and thickens. Stir in cheese and mustard.

Layer half the potato and kumara slices into prepared dishes. Pour over half the sauce. Repeat with remaining potato, kumara and sauce. Top each dish with extra cheese, nuts and paprika. Bake, uncovered, in moderate oven about 20 minutes or until heated through.

Serves 4.

- Recipe can be made a day ahead.
- Storage: Covered, in refrigerator.
- Freeze: Not suitable.
- Microwave: Potatoes, kumara and sauce suitable.

GOATS' CHEESE AND MASHED POTATO GRATIN

5 large (1.5kg) potatoes, peeled, chopped
50g butter, melted
¾ cup (90g) grated gruyere cheese
¼ cup (60ml) olive oil
3 medium (450g) onions, sliced
1 tablespoon fresh thyme leaves
100g goats' cheese

Grease 19cm x 26cm ovenproof dish (1.5 litre/6 cup capacity). Boil, steam or microwave potatoes until soft; drain. Mash potatoes with butter until smooth, stir in gruyere cheese. Heat 2 tablespoons of the oil in heavy-based pan, add onions and thyme, cook, stirring, over medium heat about 20 minutes or until onions are very soft and well browned.

Spread one-third of the onion mixture over base of prepared dish, spread with potato mixture, top with remaining onion mixture. Dot top with level teaspoons of goats' cheese, brush cheese with remaining oil. Bake in hot oven about 15 minutes or until cheese is lightly browned.

Serves 6.

- Recipe can be made a day ahead.
- Storage: Covered, in refrigerator.
- Freeze: Not suitable.
- Microwave: Potatoes suitable.

NUTTY ROASTED KUMARA AND POTATO

1 large (500g) kumara
4 medium (800g) old potatoes
1½ tablespoons olive oil
¼ cup (20g) grated parmesan cheese
2 tablespoons pine nuts
1 tablespoon chopped fresh oregano
2 teaspoons chopped fresh basil

Peel kumara and potatoes, cut into 5mm slices. Place kumara and potato slices in an overlapping layer in greased baking dish. Pour over oil, sprinkle with combined cheese, nuts and herbs. Bake in moderately hot oven about 1 hour or until kumara and potatoes are tender.

Serves 4 to 6.

- Recipe best made close to serving.
- Freeze: Not suitable.
- Microwave: Not suitable.

DUCHESSE POTATOES

4 medium (800g) old potatoes, peeled, chopped
3 egg yolks
50g soft butter
1 egg yolk, extra

Boil, steam or microwave potatoes until tender; drain. Return potatoes to pan, stir over heat 1 minute or until potatoes are very dry. Push potatoes through a sieve. Stir in egg yolks and butter; mix well. Place potato mixture into piping bag fitted with 1.5cm star tube, pipe small swirls onto greased oven trays. Brush lightly with extra egg yolk. Bake in hot oven about 10 minutes or until lightly browned.

Serves 6 to 8.

- Recipe can be prepared several hours ahead.
- Storage: Covered, in refrigerator.
- Freeze: Not suitable.
- Microwave: Potatoes suitable.

ROASTED POTATOES AND MUSHROOMS WITH OLIVES

⅓ cup (80ml) olive oil
6 unpeeled cloves garlic
5 medium (1kg) potatoes,
**   unpeeled, quartered**
6 baby (150g) onions
350g button mushrooms
1 tablespoon fresh rosemary leaves
½ cup (60g) black olives
½ cup (55g) drained sun-dried
**   tomatoes, halved**
1 tablespoon chopped fresh parsley

Combine oil, garlic, potatoes, onions, mushrooms and rosemary in large baking dish. Bake, uncovered, in hot oven, stirring occasionally, about 45 minutes or until potatoes are browned and tender. Add olives and tomatoes; mix well. Sprinkle with parsley.

Serves 6.
- Recipe best made just before serving.
- Freeze: Not suitable.
- Microwave: Not suitable.

ROASTED NEW POTATOES WITH GARLIC

20 baby (800g) new potatoes
¼ cup (60ml) virgin olive oil
12 unpeeled cloves garlic
2 tablespoons fresh rosemary leaves

Combine all ingredients in baking dish; mix well. Bake, uncovered, in moderately hot oven about 45 minutes or until potatoes are well browned and tender. Turn potatoes twice during cooking.

Serves 6.
- Recipe best made just before serving.
- Freeze: Not suitable.
- Microwave: Not suitable.

BASIC MASHED POTATO

4 medium (800g) old potatoes
40g butter
¼ cup (60ml) milk
1 teaspoon sugar

Peel potatoes and cut each into 4 even pieces. Boil, steam or microwave potatoes until tender; drain, mash well with potato masher or fork, or push potato through a sieve. Add butter, milk and sugar, beat until butter is melted.

Serves 4.
- Recipe and variations best made just before serving.
- Freeze: Not suitable.
- Microwave: Suitable.

MASHED POTATO VARIATIONS

LEEK AND THYME
1 tablespoon vegetable oil
1 small (200g) leek, sliced
1 clove garlic, crushed
1 tablespoon chopped fresh thyme
2 tablespoons dry white wine

Heat oil in pan, add leek, garlic and thyme, cook, stirring, until leek is soft. Add wine, cook, stirring, until wine is evaporated; stir leek mixture into mashed potato.

CAJUN
1 small (150g) red pepper,
**   roasted, sliced**
½ teaspoon Cajun blended spice mix
1 teaspoon chopped fresh thyme

Add pepper, spice mix and thyme to mashed potato; mix well.

ITALIAN
¼ cup (20g) grated parmesan cheese
¼ cup (40g) sliced seedless
**   black olives**
1 tablespoon chopped fresh basil

Add cheese, olives and basil to mashed potato; mix well.

PINE NUT
⅓ cup (50g) pine nuts, toasted
2 teaspoons chopped fresh rosemary

Add pine nuts and rosemary to mashed potato; mix well.

BACON AND MUSTARD
4 bacon rashers, chopped
3 teaspoons seeded mustard
1 tablespoon chopped fresh parsley

Cook bacon in pan until crisp; drain on absorbent paper. Add bacon, mustard and parsley to mashed potato; mix well.

THAI-STYLE
¼ cup (60ml) coconut cream
1 tablespoon vegetable oil
1 small (80g) onion, chopped
1 clove garlic, crushed
1 small chopped fresh chilli
1 teaspoon grated fresh ginger
1 tablespoon chopped fresh
**   coriander**

Substitute coconut cream for milk in basic mashed potato recipe. Heat oil in pan, add onion, garlic, chilli and ginger, cook, stirring, until onion is soft. Add to mashed potato with coriander; mix well.

LEFT: From back: Roasted Potatoes and Mushrooms with Olives, Roasted New Potatoes with Garlic.
RIGHT: Cajun variation of Basic Mashed Potato.

POTATO AND PEA CURRY WITH PARSLEY YOGURT

4 medium (800g) old potatoes, peeled, chopped
¼ cup (60ml) vegetable oil
1 medium (150g) onion, finely chopped
2 cloves garlic, crushed
1 teaspoon ground cumin
½ teaspoon ground coriander
½ teaspoon ground fennel
½ teaspoon ground turmeric
¼ teaspoon cayenne pepper
1 teaspoon garam masala
425g can tomatoes
1 cup (125g) frozen peas

PARSLEY YOGURT
½ cup (125ml) plain yogurt
1 tablespoon chopped fresh parsley

Boil, steam or microwave potatoes until tender. Heat oil in pan, add onion and garlic, cook, stirring, until onion is soft. Add spices and undrained crushed tomatoes, simmer, uncovered, about 5 minutes or until fragrant and slightly thickened.

Stir in potatoes, simmer, stirring occasionally, until potatoes are heated through and mixture is almost dry. Stir in peas, cook, stirring, about 3 minutes or until peas are heated through.

Parsley Yogurt: Combine ingredients in small bowl; mix well.

Serves 4 to 6.

- Parsley yogurt can be made 2 days ahead.
- Storage: Covered, in refrigerator.
- Freeze: Not suitable.
- Microwave: Curry suitable.

SPICY INDIAN-STYLE POTATOES

20 baby (800g) new potatoes, halved
¼ cup (60ml) vegetable oil
1 small (80g) onion, sliced
2 cloves garlic, crushed
2 teaspoons grated fresh ginger
1½ tablespoons mild curry powder
1 teaspoon white mustard seeds
2 teaspoons lime juice
¼ cup (60ml) water

Boil, steam or microwave potatoes until just tender; drain. Heat oil in pan, add onion, garlic and ginger, cook, stirring, until onion is soft. Add curry powder, seeds and juice, cook, stirring, until fragrant. Add potatoes and water, cook, stirring, until potatoes are heated through.

Serves 4.

- Recipe can be made a day ahead.
- Storage: Covered, in refrigerator.
- Freeze: Not suitable.
- Microwave: Potatoes suitable.

RIGHT: From left: Potato and Pea Curry with Parsley Yogurt, Spicy Indian-Style Potatoes.

POTATO, PARSNIP AND CORN PANCAKES

1 large (300g) potato
1 tablespoon vegetable oil
1 medium (125g) parsnip, grated
100g mushrooms, finely chopped
1 small (80g) onion, chopped
1⅓ cups (200g) self-raising flour
¼ teaspoon baking powder
**130g can corn kernels,
    rinsed, drained**
1 tablespoon chopped fresh rosemary
2 eggs, lightly beaten
1 cup (250ml) milk
1 tablespoon vegetable oil, extra

SOUR CREAM DRESSING
¾ cup (180ml) sour cream
3 teaspoons milk
2 teaspoons lemon juice
1 tablespoon chopped fresh chives
1 teaspoon sugar

Peel potato, cut into 1cm cubes. Heat oil in pan, add potato, parsnip, mushrooms and onion, cook, stirring, until potato is tender; cool.

Sift flour and baking powder into bowl, add potato mixture, corn and rosemary. Add combined eggs and milk, stir until just combined. Heat extra oil in pan, pour ¼ cup of mixture into pan. Cook until bubbles appear on surface and underneath is browned, turn pancake, brown other side. Repeat with remaining mixture. Serve pancakes with sour cream dressing.
Sour Cream Dressing: Combine all ingredients in bowl; mix well.

Serves 6.

- Recipe can be prepared several hours ahead.
- Storage: Covered, in refrigerator.
- Freeze: Not suitable.
- Microwave: Not suitable.

CHILLI POTATOES WITH CASHEWS AND POPPY SEEDS

**8 small (960g) potatoes,
    peeled, chopped**
1 small fresh green chilli
1 small fresh red chilli
**⅓ cup (50g) unsalted roasted
    cashew nuts**
1 tablespoon poppy seeds
60g butter

Boil, steam or microwave potatoes until just tender. Blend or process chillies, nuts and seeds until finely chopped. Heat butter in heavy-based pan, add potatoes and blended ingredients; mix well. Cook, turning potatoes occasionally, about 20 minutes or until potatoes are well-coated and crispy.

Serves 4.

- Recipe best made close to serving.
- Freeze: Not suitable.
- Microwave: Potatoes suitable.

CURRIED FRIED POTATOES AND CARROTS

**5 medium (1kg) potatoes,
    peeled, chopped**
**3 medium (360g) carrots,
    peeled, chopped**
50g butter
2 cloves garlic, crushed
1 tablespoon vegetable oil
1 tablespoon bottled red curry paste
**2 medium (260g) tomatoes, peeled,
    seeded, chopped**
½ cup (125ml) plain yogurt
**2 tablespoons chopped fresh
    coriander**

Boil, steam or microwave potatoes and carrots separately until just tender; drain. Heat butter in pan, add garlic, potatoes and carrots, cook, stirring, until potatoes are browned, remove from pan.

Heat oil in pan, add curry paste, cook, stirring, until fragrant. Add tomatoes, cook, stirring, about 3 minutes or until mixture is slightly thickened. Remove from heat, stir in potatoes, carrots, yogurt and coriander.

Serves 4 to 6.

- Recipe best made just before serving.
- Freeze: Not suitable.
- Microwave: Potatoes and carrots suitable.

LEFT: From back: Potato, Parsnip and Corn Pancakes, Chilli Potatoes with Cashews and Poppy Seeds.
BELOW: Curried Fried Potatoes and Carrots.

Left: Plate and bowl from Basic Essentials.
Below: Basket from Barbara's Storehouse.

BABY NEW POTATOES IN FOIL

50g butter, melted
1 tablespoon chopped fresh tarragon
1 tablespoon orange juice
1 teaspoon seeded mustard
1 teaspoon cranberry sauce
16 baby (640g) new potatoes

Combine butter, tarragon, juice, mustard and sauce in bowl; mix well. Add potatoes; mix well. Cover an oven tray with a 40cm x 60cm piece of foil, place potatoes in centre, bring edges of foil together, seal tightly. Bake in moderately hot oven 1 hour or until potatoes are tender.

Serves 4.

■ Recipe best made close to serving.
■ Freeze: Not suitable.
■ Microwave: Not suitable.

CRUSTY POTATO CAKE WITH CREAMY LEEK FILLING

1 tablespoon vegetable oil
40g butter, chopped
4 medium (800g) old potatoes, peeled, grated
¼ cup (20g) grated parmesan cheese

CREAMY LEEK FILLING
1 tablespoon vegetable oil
1 medium (350g) leek, finely chopped
1 medium fresh corn cob
½ cup (125ml) cream

Heat oil and half the butter in ovenproof frying pan (base measurement 18cm), add half the potatoes; press flat over base, cook, uncovered, about 5 minutes or until base is golden brown.

Spread cheese and leek filling over potato base, leaving 1cm border around edge of base. Top with remaining potato; press down evenly over filling, cook 5 minutes; remove from heat.

Gently slide potato cake onto large plate, then invert back into pan, cook further 5 minutes or until base is browned. Top with remaining butter, bake, uncovered, in moderately hot oven about 15 minutes or until tender.

Creamy Leek Filling: Heat oil in pan, add leek, cook, stirring, until leek is tender. Cut kernels from corn. Add corn and cream, cook, stirring, 5 minutes or until cream is reduced by half.

Serves 6.

■ Recipe best made close to serving.
■ Freeze: Not suitable.
■ Microwave: Not suitable.

LEFT: From back: Baby New Potatoes in Foil, Crusty Potato Cake with Creamy Leek Filling.
RIGHT: From back: Saute Potatoes with Lemon and Garlic, Potato Cakes with Coriander and Cumin.

Left: Pan and bowl from Basic Essentials.
Right: Box and serviette from Barbara's Storehouse.

POTATO CAKES WITH CORIANDER AND CUMIN

2 large (600g) old potatoes, peeled, grated
1 small (80g) onion, grated
¼ cup (40g) cornmeal
1 teaspoon ground cumin
1 teaspoon ground coriander
1 egg yolk
vegetable oil for shallow-frying

Place potatoes and onion between sheets of absorbent paper, press paper to remove as much moisture as possible. Combine potatoes, onion, cornmeal, cumin, coriander and egg yolk in bowl; mix well.

Heat oil in pan, drop level tablespoons of mixture into pan, flatten into rounds, shallow-fry on both sides until golden brown; drain on absorbent paper.

Makes about 12.

■ Recipe best made just before serving.
■ Freeze: Not suitable.
■ Microwave: Not suitable.

SAUTE POTATOES WITH LEMON AND GARLIC

5 medium (1kg) potatoes
⅓ cup (50g) cornflour
⅓ cup (25g) grated parmesan cheese
1½ tablespoons chopped fresh oregano
3 teaspoons grated lemon rind
3 cloves garlic, crushed
½ teaspoon paprika
2 tablespoons vegetable oil
40g butter

Peel potatoes, cut into 3cm pieces. Boil, steam or microwave potatoes until almost tender; drain, cool. Place potatoes in bowl, add combined cornflour, cheese, oregano, rind, garlic and paprika; mix well. Heat oil and butter in pan, add potato mixture, cook, stirring, until potatoes are browned and tender.

Serves 6.

■ Recipe best made just before serving.
■ Freeze: Not suitable.
■ Microwave: Potatoes suitable.

ROAST POTATOES WITH GARLIC AND THYME

5 large (1.5kg) old potatoes, peeled, chopped
1/3 cup (80ml) olive oil
8 cloves garlic, halved
12 sprigs fresh thyme

Cook potatoes in pan of boiling water about 10 minutes or until tender; drain. Pat potatoes dry with absorbent paper. Heat oil in a baking dish in moderately hot oven 10 minutes. Add potatoes, bake 45 minutes, add garlic and thyme; mix well. Bake further 30 minutes or until potatoes are browned. Stir potatoes occasionally during cooking.

Serves 4 to 6.

- Recipe best made close to serving.
- Freeze: Not suitable.
- Microwave: First cooking of potatoes suitable.

POTATOES ROASTED WITH BALSAMIC VINEGAR

20 small (1kg) potatoes
60g butter, melted
1/3 cup (80ml) balsamic vinegar

Peel potatoes in a spiral pattern, removing only half of the skin. Combine potatoes, butter and vinegar in baking dish; mix well. Bake potatoes in moderate oven, covered, 1 hour. Remove cover, bake further 30 minutes or until potatoes are tender. Baste potatoes several times during cooking.

Serves 6.

- Recipe best made just before serving.
- Freeze: Not suitable.
- Microwave: Not suitable.

LEEK AND POTATO SAUTE

5 medium (1kg) old potatoes, peeled
1 tablespoon olive oil
2 cloves garlic, crushed
4 bacon rashers, chopped
2 medium (700g) leeks, sliced
2 tablespoons olive oil, extra
1 teaspoon seasoned pepper

Cut potatoes into large chunks. Boil, steam or microwave potatoes until just tender; drain. Heat oil in pan, add garlic and bacon, cook, stirring, until bacon is crisp. Add leeks, cook, stirring, until leeks are soft; drain on absorbent paper.

Add extra oil to pan, add potatoes, cook, stirring occasionally, until potatoes are browned and tender. Add bacon and leek mixture and pepper, cook, stirring, until heated through.

Serves 4.

- Recipe best made close to serving.
- Freeze: Not suitable.
- Microwave: First cooking of potatoes suitable.

STEAMED POTATOES WITH GARLIC CREAM SAUCE

2 cups (500ml) water
2 cloves garlic, peeled
1/4 cup chopped fresh parsley
20 baby (800g) new potatoes

GARLIC CREAM SAUCE
20g butter
1 small (100g) red Spanish onion, chopped
1 teaspoon chopped fresh thyme
1/2 cup (125ml) creme fraiche

Boil the water in pan, add garlic and half the parsley. Place potatoes in steamer basket in pan, cover, cook about 15 minutes or until potatoes are tender. Drain, reserve garlic. Serve potatoes with garlic cream sauce.

Garlic Cream Sauce: Crush reserved garlic. Heat butter in pan, add garlic and onion, cook, stirring, until onion is soft. Stir in thyme, creme fraiche and remaining parsley; reheat without boiling.

Serves 4.

- Recipe best made just before serving.
- Freeze: Not suitable.
- Microwave: Suitable.

LEFT: From back: Potatoes Roasted with Balsamic Vinegar, Roast Potatoes with Garlic and Thyme.
RIGHT: From back: Leek and Potato Saute, Steamed Potatoes with Garlic Cream Sauce.

Left: Bowls from Kenwick Galleries.

SWISS POTATO ROSTI

**4 medium (800g) old potatoes,
  peeled, grated**
**1 medium (150g) onion,
  finely chopped**
60g butter, melted
**¼ teaspoon cracked black
  peppercorns**
2 tablespoons light olive oil

Combine potatoes, onion, butter and pepper in bowl; mix well, drain. Heat oil in pan, add ⅓ cups of potato mixture to pan; press into 10cm rounds. Cook until well browned on both sides.

Serves 4.

■ Recipe best made close to serving.
■ Freeze: Not suitable.
■ Microwave: Not suitable.

BELOW: Swiss Potato Rosti.
*RIGHT: From left: Saute Potatoes with
Tomatoes and Pancetta, Vegetable Chunks
with Dill Glaze.*
BELOW RIGHT: Winter Vegetable Curry.

Right: Basket from Barbara's Storehouse; tiles
from Perfect Ceramics. Below right: Setting from
Accoutrement.

VEGETABLE CHUNKS
WITH DILL GLAZE

1 medium (400g) kumara, peeled
2 medium (450g) swedes, peeled
1 medium (760g) celeriac, peeled
2 medium (250g) parsnips, peeled
2 medium (240g) carrots, peeled
2 cups (500ml) water
¼ cup (60ml) olive oil
2 teaspoons balsamic vinegar
1 tablespoon lemon juice
1 teaspoon sugar
2 teaspoons cornflour
1 teaspoon balsamic vinegar, extra
2 teaspoons chopped fresh dill

Chop vegetables coarsely, combine in pan with water, oil, vinegar, juice and sugar. Simmer, covered, about 10 minutes or until vegetables are tender. Strain vegetables; reserve 1 cup of cooking liquid.

Place blended reserved liquid, cornflour and extra vinegar in small pan, cook, stirring, until mixture boils and thickens; stir in dill. Serve over vegetables.

Serves 6 to 8.

■ Recipe best made close to serving.
■ Freeze: Not suitable.
■ Microwave: Suitable.

WINTER VEGETABLE CURRY

2 medium (240g) carrots
2 medium (250g) parsnips
1 medium (225g) swede
3 medium (600g) old potatoes, peeled
2 small (500g) kumara, peeled
60g ghee
2 large (400g) onions, sliced
4 cloves garlic, crushed
1 tablespoon grated fresh ginger
2 teaspoons ground coriander
2 teaspoons ground cumin
1 teaspoon ground cardamom
½ teaspoon ground cinnamon
1 teaspoon ground turmeric
½ teaspoon chilli powder
2 x 425g cans tomatoes
2 tablespoons plain yogurt

Cut carrots, parsnips, swede, potatoes and kumara into 2cm pieces. Heat ghee in pan, add onions, garlic and ginger, cook, stirring, until onions are soft. Add spices, cook, stirring, until fragrant.

Add chopped vegetables to pan, stir in undrained crushed tomatoes, simmer, covered, 15 minutes. Remove lid, simmer, stirring occasionally, further 30 minutes or until vegetables are tender. Stir in yogurt.

Serves 4 to 6.

■ Recipe can be made a day ahead.
■ Storage: Covered, in refrigerator.
■ Freeze: Not suitable.
■ Microwave: Suitable.

SAUTE POTATOES WITH TOMATOES AND PANCETTA

2 tablespoons olive oil
18 baby (720g) new potatoes,
    quartered
150g pancetta, chopped
1 medium (150g) onion, sliced
2 cloves garlic, crushed
425g can tomatoes
1 teaspoon sugar
¼ cup shredded fresh basil

Heat oil in frying pan, add potatoes, cook, stirring, until browned and tender; remove from pan. Add pancetta to same pan with onion and garlic, cook, stirring, until onion is soft. Return potatoes to pan with undrained crushed tomatoes and sugar, simmer, uncovered, about 5 minutes or until slightly thickened; stir in basil.

Serves 4 to 6.

■ Recipe can be made a day ahead.
■ Storage: Covered, in refrigerator.
■ Freeze: Not suitable.
■ Microwave: Not suitable.

SPICED CAULIFLOWER, PEAS AND POTATOES

3 medium (600g) potatoes, peeled
½ small (500g) cauliflower, chopped
1 tablespoon vegetable oil
1 medium (150g) onion, sliced
1 clove garlic, crushed
1 teaspoon grated fresh ginger
2 small fresh red chillies, seeded, chopped
3 teaspoons black mustard seeds
2 teaspoons cumin seeds
½ teaspoon ground turmeric
1½ cups (185g) frozen peas
½ cup (125ml) coconut milk
1 tablespoon chopped fresh coriander

Cut potatoes into 2cm pieces. Boil, steam or microwave potatoes and cauliflower separately until almost tender; drain. Heat oil in pan, add onion, garlic, ginger and chillies, cook, stirring, until onion is soft.

Add seeds and turmeric, cook, stirring, until fragrant. Stir in potatoes, cauliflower, peas and milk, cook, stirring, until heated through. Sprinkle with coriander.

Serves 4 to 6.

■ Recipe can be made a day ahead.
■ Storage: Covered, in refrigerator.
■ Freeze: Not suitable.
■ Microwave: Potatoes and cauliflower suitable.

POTATOES WITH GINGER CHIPS

3 large (900g) new potatoes
vegetable oil for deep-frying
¼ cup (60ml) olive oil
1 tablespoon grated fresh ginger
1 clove garlic, crushed

GINGER CHIPS
2 x 5cm pieces (80g) fresh ginger
¼ cup (40g) icing sugar mixture

Cut unpeeled potatoes into 7cm lengths. Deep-fry potatoes in batches in hot vegetable oil until well-browned all over and cooked through; drain on absorbent paper. Place potatoes in baking dish, pour over combined olive oil, ginger and garlic, cook, uncovered, in hot oven about 15 minutes or until heated through. Add ginger chips; toss to combine.

Ginger Chips: Using a vegetable peeler, peel thin strips from ginger, toss in icing sugar. Deep-fry ginger chips in batches in hot oil until lightly browned; drain on absorbent paper.

Serves 4.

■ Recipe best made just before serving.
■ Freeze: Not suitable.
■ Microwave: Not suitable.

BASIC POTATO GRATIN

Do not use thickened cream.

1 bulb (70g) garlic
5 large (1.5kg) old potatoes, peeled
1½ cups (185g) grated gruyere cheese
300ml cream
¼ teaspoon ground nutmeg

Grease 23cm square slab cake pan. Place garlic on oven tray, bake in moderately hot oven about 50 minutes or until garlic is very soft. Cool 10 minutes, cut in half, squeeze out garlic; mash.

Cut potatoes into 3mm slices. Layer potatoes in prepared pan, sprinkling with two-thirds of the cheese between layers. Combine cream, garlic and nutmeg in small bowl, pour mixture over potatoes; top with remaining cheese.

Bake, uncovered, in moderately hot oven about 1½ hours or until potatoes are tender and top is well browned. Every 30 minutes, press potatoes down into cream mixture with an eggslice.

Serves 6 to 8.

■ Recipes best made on day of serving.
■ Storage: Covered, in refrigerator.
■ Freeze: Not suitable.
■ Microwave: Not suitable.

GRATIN VARIATIONS

ONION, CHEESE AND POTATO

40g butter
4 medium (600g) onions, finely sliced
¼ cup (20g) grated parmesan cheese
¼ cup (30g) grated gruyere cheese
5 large (1.5kg) old potatoes, peeled
¾ cup (180ml) chicken stock
¼ teaspoon ground nutmeg

Prepare pan as for basic potato gratin. Heat butter in large pan, add onions, cook over low heat about 15 minutes or until onions are very soft; cool. Combine cheeses with onion mixture; mix well.

Cut potatoes into 3mm slices. Layer potatoes in prepared pan, sprinkling with onion mixture between layers, finishing with potatoes. Pour combined stock and nutmeg over potatoes, sprinkle with remaining cheese.

Bake, uncovered, in moderately hot oven about 1 hour and 40 minutes or until potatoes are tender and most of the liquid is evaporated.

PROSCIUTTO AND PINE NUT
Do not use thickened cream.

1 bulb (70g) garlic
2 tablespoons olive oil
1 large (500g) leek, finely chopped
100g shitake mushrooms,
finely chopped
1 tablespoon chopped fresh rosemary
100g prosciutto, chopped
½ cup (80g) pine nuts, toasted
2 tablespoons finely chopped,
drained sun-dried tomatoes
5 large (1.5kg) old potatoes, peeled
⅓ cup (25g) finely grated parmesan
cheese
300ml cream

Prepare pan and garlic as for basic potato gratin. Heat oil in pan, add leek, mushrooms, rosemary and prosciutto, cook, stirring occasionally, about 10 minutes or until leek is soft; cool 10 minutes. Stir in nuts and tomatoes.

Cut potatoes into 3mm slices. Layer potatoes in prepared pan, sprinkling leek mixture between layers, finishing with potatoes; sprinkle with cheese. Pour over combined cream and garlic.

Bake, uncovered, in moderately hot oven about 1½ hours or until potatoes are tender and top well browned. Every 30 minutes, press potatoes down into cream mixture with an eggslice.

KUMARA, POTATO AND THYME
Do not use thickened cream.

1 bulb (70g) garlic
6 medium (1.2kg) old potatoes, peeled
2 medium (800g) kumara, peeled
1 cup (80g) grated parmesan cheese
2 tablespoons chopped fresh thyme
300ml cream

Prepare pan and garlic as for basic potato gratin. Cut potatoes and kumara into 3mm slices. Layer half the potatoes in prepared pan, sprinkle with some of the combined cheese and thyme. Top with all the kumara, sprinkle with more cheese and thyme. Add remaining potato, sprinkle with remaining cheese and thyme. Pour over combined cream and garlic.

Bake, uncovered, in moderately hot oven about 1½ hours or until potatoes are tender and top is well browned. Every 30 minutes, press potatoes down into cream mixture with an eggslice.

LEFT: From left: Potatoes with Ginger Chips, Spiced Cauliflower, Peas and Potatoes.
ABOVE: Prosciutto and Pine Nut variation of Basic Potato Gratin.

Breads & Sweet Surprises

If the thought of using potatoes and kumara in sweet recipes and breads is unfamiliar to you, it soon won't be! There are treats as surprising as an extravagant chocolate truffle cake, a nutty kumara pie, doughnuts, waffles and lunchbox cakes. The breads are wonderful, too, with diverse flavours, including focaccia and rolls with a tasty filling.

MOIST CHOCOLATE POTATO TRUFFLE CAKE

¼ cup (60ml) brandy
⅓ cup (55g) seedless prunes, finely chopped
125g soft butter
1½ cups (300g) brown sugar, firmly packed
2 eggs, lightly beaten
1¾ cups (255g) self-raising flour
½ cup (50g) cocoa
¾ cup (180ml) water
1 medium (200g) old potato, peeled, grated

TRUFFLE PRUNE FILLING
¾ cup (180ml) cream
200g dark chocolate, finely chopped
1 egg yolk
2 tablespoons brandy
2 tablespoons finely chopped seedless prunes

Line base and side of deep 22cm round cake pan with a layer of baking paper, bringing paper 5cm above edge of pan. Combine brandy and prunes in small bowl; stand 30 minutes.

Beat butter and sugar in medium bowl with electric mixer until light and fluffy. Add eggs 1 at a time, beat until combined. Stir in sifted flour and cocoa, prune mixture, water and potato in 2 batches.

Pour mixture into prepared pan, bake in moderate oven about 1¼ hours. Stand cake 5 minutes before turning onto wire rack to cool.

Line base and side of same clean cake pan with plastic wrap. Level top of cake. Split cake into 2 layers. Place 1 layer into pan, spread with partly set filling, top with remaining layer. Cover, refrigerate until filling is set. Turn out carefully onto serving plate; dust with extra cocoa, if desired.

Truffle Prune Filling: Bring cream to boil in small pan, remove from heat; add chocolate, stir until smooth and melted. Stir in egg yolk, brandy and prunes. Refrigerate until thick, stirring occasionally so that mixture thickens evenly.

Serves 10.

- Cake can be made a day ahead.
- Storage: Covered, in refrigerator.
- Freeze: Unfilled cake suitable.
- Microwave: Filling suitable.

RIGHT: Moist Chocolate Potato Truffle Cake.

MINT COCONUT ROUGHS

**1 medium (200g) potato,
  peeled, chopped**
40g soft butter
1¼ cups (200g) icing sugar mixture
1½ cups (135g) coconut
few drops peppermint oil
few drops green food colouring
1½ tablespoons cocoa

Boil, steam or microwave potato until tender, drain; mash. Push potato through a sieve. You will need ½ cup mashed potato for this recipe. While potato is still warm, add butter; mix well.

Stir in sifted icing sugar and coconut. Add peppermint oil and food colouring to ⅓ cup of coconut mixture; mix well. Add cocoa to remaining coconut mixture; mix well.

Roll level teaspoons of peppermint mixture into balls. Flatten 1 tablespoon of the chocolate mixture in palm of hand, top with a peppermint ball and bring chocolate around ball to enclose peppermint mixture. Repeat with remaining peppermint and chocolate mixtures. Roll mint coconut roughs in drinking chocolate or shredded coconut, if desired.

Makes about 15.

- Recipe can be made several hours ahead.
- Storage: Covered, in refrigerator.
- Freeze: Not suitable.
- Microwave: Potato suitable.

CHERRY COCONUT ICE

You will need to cook 1 medium (200g) potato for this recipe.

½ cup mashed potato
3 cups (270g) coconut
3 cups (480g) icing sugar mixture
75g Copha, melted
2 egg whites
**¼ cup (60g) red glace cherries,
  chopped**
few drops red food colouring

Grease 15cm x 25cm loaf pan. Push mashed potato through a sieve. Combine potato, coconut and sifted icing sugar in large bowl, beat with electric mixer until combined; add Copha and firmly beaten egg whites, beat until well combined.

Press half the mixture over base of prepared pan. Add cherries and colouring to remaining mixture, press evenly over white mixture. Refrigerate until set.

Makes about 32.

- Recipe can be made 3 days ahead.
- Storage: Covered, in refrigerator.
- Freeze: Not suitable.
- Microwave: Potato suitable.

COCONUT ICE VARIATION

CHOC ORANGE
Omit cherries and food colouring. Add 2 teaspoons grated orange rind to potato mixture. Press half the mixture over base of prepared pan. Add 50g melted dark chocolate to remaining mixture; proceed as above.

POTATO ALMOND STRUDEL

You will need to cook 2 medium (400g) potatoes for this recipe.

8 sheets fillo pastry
60g butter, melted

FILLING
1 cup cold mashed potato
4 egg yolks
½ cup (110g) caster sugar
**2 cups (250g) packaged ground
  almonds**
2 teaspoons grated lemon rind
½ cup (95g) mixed dried fruit

Layer pastry sheets together, brushing each with butter. Shape filling into a 10cm x 25cm rectangle along centre of pastry. Fold in short ends; roll over to enclose filling. Place strudel on greased oven tray, seam side down, brush with butter, bake in moderate oven about 40 minutes or until strudel is browned. Serve strudel warm or cold, dusted with sifted icing sugar, if desired.

Filling: Push potato through fine sieve. Beat yolks and sugar in small bowl with electric mixer until pale and thick. Stir in potato, nuts, rind and fruit.

Serves 6.

- Strudel can be made a day ahead.
- Storage: Covered, in refrigerator.
- Freeze: Not suitable.
- Microwave: Potatoes suitable.

ABOVE: Clockwise from left: Cherry Coconut Ice, Choc Orange Coconut Ice, Mint Coconut Roughs.

KUMARA AND ZUCCHINI LOAF

2 eggs
1 cup (200g) firmly packed brown sugar
½ cup (125ml) buttermilk
125g butter, melted
½ cup (70g) grated zucchini
1 cup (135g) grated kumara
½ cup (85g) dates, finely chopped
½ cup (50g) pecans, chopped
¾ cup (120g) wholemeal plain flour
1½ cups (225g) white self-raising flour
½ cup (75g) white plain flour
1 teaspoon mixed spice
1 teaspoon ground cinnamon

Grease 15cm x 25cm loaf pan, cover base with baking paper. Whisk eggs, sugar, milk and butter in bowl until combined. Stir in vegetables, dates and nuts. Stir in sifted dry ingredients in 2 batches. Spread mixture into prepared pan. Bake in moderate oven about 1 hour and 10 minutes. Turn loaf onto wire rack to cool. Serve loaf with butter, if desired.

■ Loaf can be made several days ahead.
■ Storage: Airtight container.
■ Freeze: Suitable.
■ Microwave: Not suitable.

OATY CHEESE AND MUSTARD ROLLS

1 medium (200g) old potato,
  peeled, chopped
1¼ cups (185g) white
  self-raising flour
½ cup (80g) wholemeal
  self-raising flour
½ cup (60g) grated tasty
  cheddar cheese
1 tablespoon seeded mustard
40g butter, melted
⅔ cup (160ml) milk, approximately
¼ cup (20g) grated parmesan cheese
¼ cup (20g) rolled oats

Grease 23cm round sandwich cake pan. Boil, steam or microwave potato until tender; drain, mash, cool. Sift flours into bowl, add potato, tasty cheese and mustard. Stir in butter and enough milk to mix to a soft sticky dough. Turn dough onto floured surface, divide dough into 12 portions.

Knead each portion lightly to form a round shape, place in prepared pan. Bake in very hot oven 10 minutes, sprinkle with combined parmesan cheese and oats, bake further 10 minutes or until browned and cooked through.

Makes 12.

■ Recipe best made on day of serving.
■ Freeze: Suitable.
■ Microwave: Potato suitable.

LEFT: Potato Almond Strudel.
ABOVE: From left: Oaty Cheese and Mustard Rolls, Kumara and Zucchini Loaf.

Above: Basket from The Bay Tree Kitchen Shop.

KUMARA CUSTARDS WITH ORANGE CREAM

You will need to cook 1 medium (400g) kumara for this recipe.

1 cup cold mashed kumara
⅓ cup (75g) caster sugar
1 egg
2 egg yolks
½ teaspoon mixed spice
½ teaspoon grated orange rind
⅔ cup (160ml) cream
8 fresh dates, seeded, halved
2 medium (360g) oranges, segmented
ORANGE CREAM
½ cup (125ml) sour cream
2 teaspoons Grand Marnier
2 teaspoons icing sugar mixture

Push kumara through a fine sieve. Whisk sugar, egg, egg yolks, spice and rind in bowl until combined. Whisk in kumara and cream. Divide mixture evenly between 4 ovenproof dishes (⅔ cup/ 160ml capacity).

Place dishes in baking dish with enough boiling water to come halfway up sides of ovenproof dishes. Bake, un-covered, in moderate oven about 1 hour or until knife comes out clean when inserted into centre of custards; cool, refrigerate until cold. Serve kumara custards with orange cream, dates and orange segments; dust with sifted icing sugar, if desired.
Orange Cream: Combine all ingredients in bowl; mix well.

Serves 4.

- Custards and orange cream can be made a day ahead.
- Storage: Covered, separately, in refrigerator.
- Freeze: Not suitable.
- Microwave: Kumara suitable.

KUMARA, ORANGE AND WALNUT DOUGHNUTS

You will need to cook about 1½ medium (600g) kumara for this recipe. Cut doughnuts in batches, re-rolling dough as necessary.

½ cup (60g) walnuts
2½ cups (375g) self-raising flour
½ cup (75g) potato flour
1 teaspoon ground cinnamon
¼ teaspoon ground nutmeg
¾ cup (165g) brown sugar
1 teaspoon grated orange rind
2 eggs
50g butter, melted
2 tablespoons Grand Marnier
⅓ cup (80ml) plain yogurt
1½ cups mashed kumara
vegetable oil for deep-frying
½ cup (110g) caster sugar
1½ teaspoons ground
cinnamon, extra

Process nuts until finely ground. Sift flours and spices into large bowl, add brown sugar, nuts and rind; mix well.

In a separate bowl, combine eggs, but-ter, liqueur, yogurt and kumara; beat until smooth. Stir kumara mixture into flour mixture, mix to a soft dough. Knead dough on lightly floured surface about 5 minutes or until smooth, adding more flour if mix-ture becomes too sticky. Roll dough until 8mm thick.

Cut dough into 7cm rounds; cut a 2cm hole from centre of each round. Place doughnuts on oven trays, refrigerate 20 minutes or until firm.

Deep-fry doughnuts in hot oil until browned; drain on absorbent paper. Roll doughnuts in combined caster sugar and extra cinnamon.

Makes about 35.

- Dough can be made 2 hours ahead.
- Storage: Airtight container.
- Freeze: Unsuitable.
- Microwave: Kumara suitable.

GOLDEN KUMARA WAFFLES

You will need to cook 1 medium (400g) kumara for this recipe.

60g butter
¼ cup (60ml) water
2 tablespoons brown sugar
2 tablespoons golden syrup
2 eggs, separated
½ cup (125ml) milk
1 cup (150g) plain flour
1 cup mashed kumara

Combine butter, water, sugar and golden syrup in pan, stir over heat, without boil-ing, until sugar is dissolved. Bring to boil, without stirring, remove from heat; cool.

Transfer mixture to bowl, stir in egg yolks, milk, then sifted flour and kumara; beat until smooth. Beat egg whites in small bowl with electric mixer until soft peaks form; gently fold into batter.

Drop about ⅓ cup of mixture into heated greased waffle iron. Close iron, cook about 1 minute or until waffle is browned. Repeat with remaining batter. Serve waffles with maple syrup and ice-cream, if desired.

Makes about 8.

- Recipe best made just before serving.
- Freeze: Suitable.
- Microwave: Kumara suitable.

LEFT: Clockwise from back: Kumara, Orange and Walnut Doughnuts, Kumara Custards with Orange Cream, Golden Kumara Waffles.

KUMARA, ORANGE AND GINGER SOUFFLES

200g kumara, peeled, chopped
1 tablespoon glace ginger,
   finely chopped
pinch ground nutmeg
½ teaspoon ground cinnamon
1 teaspoon grated orange rind
2 tablespoons brown sugar
2 tablespoons plain flour
2 egg yolks
5 egg whites
2 tablespoons caster sugar

ORANGE CREAM
300ml rich cream
2 tablespoons icing sugar mixture
2 teaspoons grated orange rind
1½ tablespoons Grand Marnier

Grease 4 ovenproof dishes (1¼ cup/ 310ml capacity), dust bases and sides with a little extra caster sugar, shake away excess sugar. Boil, steam or microwave kumara until tender; drain, cool 10 minutes in strainer, mash.

Combine ginger, spices, rind, brown sugar, flour, egg yolks and kumara in large bowl; mix well. Beat egg whites in bowl with electric mixer until soft peaks form, gradually add the caster sugar, continue beating until sugar is dissolved. Gently fold egg white mixture into kumara mixture in 2 batches.

Spoon mixture evenly into prepared dishes, level tops using a knife. Lightly run knife around outer edge of souffle against rim of dish (this will prevent souffle from sticking to side when rising). Place souffles on oven tray. Bake in moderately hot oven about 20 minutes or until puffed. Serve immediately with orange cream.

Orange Cream: Combine all ingredients in small bowl; mix well.

Serves 4.

- Souffles must be made just before serving. Orange cream can be made a day ahead.
- Storage: Covered, in refrigerator.
- Freeze: Not suitable.
- Microwave: Kumara suitable.

BELOW: Kumara, Orange and Ginger Souffles.
RIGHT: From back: Lime and Kumara Butter Cake, Roast Kumara, Peanut and Raisin Loaf.

Right: Plate from Corso De' Fiori.

ROAST KUMARA, PEANUT AND RAISIN LOAF

1 medium (400g) kumara
1¾ cups (255g) plain flour
1 teaspoon bicarbonate of soda
2 teaspoons mixed spice
½ teaspoon ground nutmeg
1 tablespoon finely chopped
   glace ginger
¾ cup (120g) raisins, chopped
1 cup (220g) caster sugar
½ cup (125ml) peanut oil
1 teaspoon vanilla essence
2 eggs, lightly beaten
¼ cup (60ml) orange juice
2 tablespoons roasted unsalted
   peanuts, chopped

Grease base and sides of 15cm x 25cm loaf pan, cover base with baking paper. Using a skewer, prick kumara several times, place on oven tray. Bake in moderate oven about 1 hour or until tender; cool 15 minutes. Peel and mash kumara; cool. You will need 1 cup mashed kumara for this recipe.

Sift flour, soda, spice and nutmeg into bowl; stir in ginger, raisins and sugar. Stir in oil, essence, eggs, juice and kumara; mix well. Spoon mixture into prepared pan, sprinkle with nuts. Bake in moderate oven about 1 hour. Stand loaf in pan 10 minutes before turning onto wire rack to cool.

- Recipe can be made 2 days ahead.
- Storage: Airtight container.
- Freeze: Suitable.
- Microwave: Not suitable.

LIME AND KUMARA BUTTER CAKE

1 small (250g) kumara, peeled, chopped
125g soft butter
1 teaspoon grated lime rind
⅔ cup (150g) caster sugar
2 eggs
1½ cups (225g) self-raising flour
¼ cup (35g) plain flour
¼ cup (60ml) milk

Grease 20cm ring cake pan, cover base with baking paper. Boil, steam or microwave kumara until tender; drain, mash; cool. You need ¾ cup kumara in this recipe. Cream butter, rind and sugar in small bowl with electric mixer until light and fluffy, beat in eggs 1 at a time; beat until combined. Transfer mixture to large bowl.

Stir in kumara, sifted flours and milk; mix well. Spread mixture into prepared pan. Bake in moderate oven about 40 minutes. Cool on wire rack. Sprinkle with sifted icing sugar, if desired.

- Recipe can be made a day ahead.
- Storage: Airtight container.
- Freeze: Suitable.
- Microwave: Kumara suitable.

SESAME POTATO BREAD

2 medium (400g) potatoes
3 cups (450g) plain flour
⅓ cup (50g) sesame seeds, toasted
2 teaspoons (7g) dried yeast
1 tablespoon brown sugar
1 teaspoon salt
2 tablespoons chopped fresh chives
1 cup (250ml) warm milk
1 tablespoon vegetable oil
1 egg, lightly beaten
1 teaspoon sesame seeds,
   toasted, extra

Grease 14cm x 21cm loaf pan, line base and 2 opposite sides with baking paper. Peel potatoes, cut into 1cm cubes. Boil, steam or microwave potatoes until tender; drain, cool.

Sift flour into large bowl, add potatoes, seeds, yeast, sugar, salt and chives. Stir in milk and oil, mix to a soft dough. Knead dough on floured surface about 10 minutes or until dough is smooth and elastic. Place dough in oiled bowl, cover; stand in warm place about 1 hour or until dough is doubled in size.

Turn dough onto floured surface, knead until smooth. Divide dough into 2 portions,

knead each portion into a rounded shape. Place both portions in prepared pan, stand in warm place about 30 minutes or until dough is almost doubled in size. Brush loaf with egg, sprinkle with extra sesame seeds, bake in moderate oven about 40 minutes or until loaf sounds hollow when tapped.

- Recipe best made on day of serving.
- Storage: Airtight container.
- Freeze: Not suitable.
- Microwave: Potatoes suitable.

POTATO ROLLS WITH HERBED BACON FILLING

You will need to cook 2 medium (400g) potatoes or 1 medium (400g) kumara for this recipe.

1¾ cups (430ml) milk
30g compressed yeast
1kg bread flour
1 tablespoon salt
1 tablespoon caster sugar
¾ cup (180ml) water
50g butter, melted

HERBED BACON FILLING
30g butter
1 bacon rasher, finely chopped
1 clove garlic, crushed
1 teaspoon chopped fresh thyme
1 cup mashed potato or kumara
1 tablespoon chopped fresh chives

Grease 2 oven trays. Bring milk to boil, cool to room temperature; add crumbled yeast, stir until dissolved. Sift dry ingredients into large bowl, stir in yeast mixture, water and butter; mix to a soft dough. Knead dough on floured surface about 10 minutes or until dough is smooth and elastic. Place dough in oiled bowl, cover; stand in warm place about 45 minutes or until dough is doubled in size.

Turn dough onto lightly floured surface, knead until smooth; divide dough evenly into 24 portions, shape each portion using the following methods, if desired.

Long Rolls: Roll each portion of dough to 15cm rectangle, place 2 teaspoons of filling 5cm from 1 end of dough, roll up and place on prepared trays, cover; stand in warm place about 15 minutes or until doubled in size.

Round Rolls: Roll each portion of dough to 10cm round, place 2 teaspoons of filling in centre of each round, pinch dough up to enclose filling. Place rounds, pinched side down, onto prepared trays, cover; stand in warm place about 15 minutes or until doubled in size.

To decorate, sprinkle with a little extra flour and slash surface with a knife; or brush with beaten egg and sprinkle with sesame or poppy seeds. Bake in hot oven about 20 minutes.

Herbed Bacon Filling: Heat butter in pan, add bacon, garlic and thyme, cook 3 minutes. Combine bacon mixture, potato and chives in bowl.

Makes 24.

- Recipe best made on day of serving.
- Storage: Airtight container.
- Freeze: Cooked rolls suitable.
- Microwave: Potato and kumara suitable.

LEFT: From back: Sesame Potato Bread, Potato Rolls with Herbed Bacon Filling.
RIGHT: Kumara Nut Pie.

Right: Yellow plate and cake slice from The Bay Tree Kitchen Shop; coffee cups and saucers from Corso De' Fiori.

KUMARA NUT PIE

90g soft butter
¼ cup (55g) caster sugar
1 egg, lightly beaten
1¼ cups (185g) plain flour
¼ cup (35g) self-raising flour
¼ cup (30g) chopped pecans
¾ cup (75g) pecan halves, extra

FILLING
1 large (500g) kumara, peeled, chopped
¾ cup (150g) firmly packed brown sugar
½ teaspoon ground ginger
1 teaspoon ground cinnamon
2 tablespoons maple syrup
4 eggs, lightly beaten
3 teaspoons grated orange rind
¼ cup (60ml) cream

Grease 23cm round x 3.5cm deep loose-base flan tin. Beat butter in small bowl with electric mixer until smooth, add sugar and egg, beat only until combined; do not overbeat. Stir in half the sifted flours with wooden spoon, then remaining flours and chopped nuts by hand. Knead gently on lightly floured surface until smooth. Wrap in plastic; refrigerate 30 minutes. Roll pastry between sheets of baking paper until large enough to line prepared tin. Lift pastry into tin, ease into side, trim edge. Lightly prick pastry with fork; refrigerate 30 minutes.

Cover pastry with baking paper, fill with dried beans or rice. Place on oven tray, bake in moderately hot oven 10 minutes. Remove paper and beans carefully from pastry case, bake further 10 minutes or until browned; cool.

Pour filling into pastry case, place on oven tray, bake in moderately hot oven 20 minutes. Place extra nuts around edge of pie, return to oven, reduce heat to moderate, bake further 25 minutes or until pie is firm.

Filling: Boil, steam or microwave kumara until tender; drain, push through sieve. Combine kumara, sugar, spices, syrup, eggs, rind and cream in bowl; mix well.

Serves 6 to 8.

- Recipe can be made 2 days ahead.
- Storage: Covered, in refrigerator.
- Freeze: Not suitable.
- Microwave: Kumara suitable.

POTATO AND CARAWAY SCONES

1 clove garlic
1 large (300g) potato, peeled, chopped
2 cups (300g) self-raising flour
2 teaspoons caraway seeds
1 teaspoon dry mustard
2 tablespoons chopped fresh chives
1/3 cup (25g) grated parmesan cheese
2 tablespoons olive oil
3/4 cup (180ml) buttermilk

Grease 20cm round sandwich cake pan. Flatten garlic by pressing with the side of a knife. Boil, steam or microwave potato with garlic until just tender; drain, discard garlic; cool.

Sift flour into bowl, stir in seeds, mustard, chives, potato and all but 1 tablespoon of the cheese. Stir in combined oil and buttermilk, mix to a soft dough. Turn dough onto lightly floured surface, knead lightly until smooth.

Roll dough out to 2.5cm thickness, cut into 12 x 5cm rounds. Place scones in prepared pan, sprinkle with remaining cheese. Bake in very hot oven about 20 minutes or until risen and browned.

Makes 12.

▦ Recipe can be made 3 hours ahead.
▦ Freeze: Suitable.
▦ Microwave: Potato suitable.

BUTTERMILK KUMARA DAMPER

You will need to cook 1 medium (400g) kumara for this recipe.

3 cups (450g) self-raising flour
1/2 teaspoon salt
1 tablespoon caster sugar
1 teaspoon mixed spice
30g butter
1 cup mashed kumara
1 cup (250ml) buttermilk
1/4 cup (60ml) water, approximately

Sift dry ingredients into bowl, rub in butter, make well in centre, add kumara, buttermilk and enough water to mix to a soft, sticky dough. Turn dough onto lightly floured surface; knead lightly until smooth.

Press dough into 18cm round, place on greased oven tray. Cut a cross through top of dough, about 1cm deep. Brush dough with a little extra milk, dust with a little extra flour. Bake in hot oven about 40 minutes or until damper sounds hollow when tapped.

Makes 1.

▦ Recipe best made just before serving.
▦ Freeze: Suitable.
▦ Microwave: Kumara suitable.

POTATO AND ROSEMARY FOCACCIA

1 large (300g) potato, peeled, chopped
1 tablespoon (14g) dried yeast
1/2 cup (125ml) warm water
4 cups (600g) plain flour
2 teaspoons salt
1/2 cup (125ml) warm milk
1/4 cup (60ml) olive oil
1 tablespoon fresh rosemary leaves

TOPPING
1 large (300g) potato, peeled, chopped
2 cloves garlic, crushed
30g butter
1 tablespoon cream
1 tablespoon finely chopped fresh rosemary

Grease 26cm x 32cm Swiss roll pan. Boil, steam or microwave potato until tender; drain, mash, cool. Combine yeast and water in small bowl, stand in warm place about 10 minutes or until mixture is frothy.

Sift flour and salt into large bowl, rub in mashed potato. Stir in yeast mixture and milk, mix to a firm dough. Knead dough on floured surface about 5 minutes or until dough is smooth and elastic. Place dough in oiled bowl, cover; stand in warm place about 1 1/2 hours or until doubled in size.

Turn dough onto floured surface, knead until smooth. Press dough into prepared pan, cover; stand in warm place about 1 hour or until doubled in size.

Spoon topping into piping bag fitted with small plain tube, pipe topping in a diagonal lattice pattern across top of dough. Lightly brush dough with oil and sprinkle with rosemary leaves. Bake in moderate oven about 1 hour or until well browned. Cool in pan.

Topping: Boil, steam or microwave potato until tender, drain; mash with garlic, butter, cream and rosemary until smooth, cool before using.

Serves 4 to 6.

▦ Recipe best made on day of serving.
▦ Freeze: Not suitable.
▦ Microwave: Potatoes suitable.

LEFT: From back: Buttermilk Kumara Damper, Potato and Caraway Scones.

RIGHT: From back: Dill and Potato Bread, Potato and Rosemary Focaccia.

Right: Breadboard and basket from Country Furniture Antiques; wicker platter from Accoutrement.

ILL AND POTATO BREAD

ou will need to cook 2 medium 400g) old potatoes for this recipe.

- teaspoons (10g) dried yeast
- teaspoon caster sugar
- 3 cup (80ml) warm buttermilk
- 3 cup (80ml) warm water
- 1/4 cups (485g) plain flour
- teaspoon salt
- 0g soft butter
- cup mashed potato
- cloves garlic, crushed
- tablespoons chopped fresh dill

Grease 14cm x 21cm loaf pan. Combine yeast with sugar in small bowl, stir in milk and water, cover; stand in warm place about 10 minutes or until mixture is frothy.

Sift flour and salt into large bowl, rub in butter and potato. Stir in yeast mixture, garlic and dill, mix to a firm dough. Knead dough on floured surface about 5 minutes or until dough is smooth and elastic. Place dough in oiled bowl, cover; stand in warm place about 1 hour or until dough is doubled in size. Turn dough onto lightly floured surface, knead until smooth.

Shape dough into a loaf, place into prepared pan, cover; stand in warm place about 30 minutes or until doubled in size.

Cut 3 x 5mm deep slits on top of loaf. Bake in hot oven 10 minutes, reduce heat to moderate, bake further 30 minutes or until loaf sounds hollow when tapped. Cool loaf on wire rack before serving.

Makes 1.

- ■ Recipe best made on day of serving.
- ■ Storage: Airtight container.
- ■ Freeze: Suitable.
- ■ Microwave: Potato suitable.

KNOW YOUR POTATOES

Potato flesh is either white or cream-yellow, depending on the variety. Yellow-fleshed varieties generally have a smooth, creamy texture (sometimes referred to as "waxy"). White varieties vary from smooth to a dry, floury texture. Dry potatoes are generally better for frying (chipping), whereas the moister potatoes are best for boiling.

OLD AND NEW

All varieties produce both "old" and "new" potatoes, depending on how soon they are harvested and used after the plants are fully grown. Old potatoes are either left in the ground or stored for some time after the plants mature.

NUTRITIONAL VALUE

The potato is 99.9 per cent fat free. There are 367 kilojoules (90 calories) in a medium (200g) potato – about the same as an apple. It is the added extras – such as butter, cream and gravy – that make the potato fattening, plus the fats and oils they are cooked in. Potatoes are an excellent source of easily digested carbohydrates plus minerals such as iron, magnesium, potassium, and essential vitamins such as vitamin C and several B group vitamins. Potatoes also contain a small quantity of protein.

BUYING

Potatoes can be sold either washed, or unwashed and brushed. Washed potatoes are best used soon after purchase. Unwashed potatoes are generally best for storage. Choose potatoes that are firm, dry and free of blemishes. Never buy green-skinned potatoes; they can be toxic.

STORING

Store in a cool, dark, dry place (not the refrigerator). Warmth makes potatoes sprout, damp causes rot, and light turns potatoes green. Avoid storing near strong-smelling food or commodities. Potatoes with small sprouts can be used; rub off or peel away the sprouts.

PREPARING

Peel thinly; thick peeling is wasteful and loses nutrients under the skin. Peel just before required; potatoes lose nutritive value if left soaking in water. Before boiling, cut into even-sized pieces so they will cook at the same time, saving fuel.

COOKING

Always boil gently, or steam them. Potatoes also cook well in a microwave oven, either in their jackets or peeled; follow the oven manufacturer's instructions. Our recipes give many delicious ways to cook potatoes.

ATLANTIC: Medium-sized, round potato. Rough skin, white flesh. Most suitable for deep-frying as chips. Only fair for boiling.

BINTJE: Oblong to long potato. Cream skin, yellow flesh. Excellent for salads. Suitable for boiling, mashing and frying.

COLIBAN: Medium-sized, round potato. White skin, white flesh. Most suitable for baking, roasting and mashing. Not suitable for frying or salads.

DESIREE: Long, oval potato. Smooth pink skin, yellow flesh. Most suitable for salads, roasting, boiling and mashing. Not suitable for frying.

KENNEBEC: Medium to large, oval potato. White skin, white flesh. Excellent for frying. Suitable for mashing, baking, roasting. Not suitable for salads.

KIPFLER: Small to medium, elongated potato. Yellow skin, yellow flesh. Excellent for salads. Suitable for roasting, baking and mashing. Not suitable for frying.

NICOLA: Medium-sized, oval potato. Cream skin, firm yellow flesh. Most suitable for boiling and mashing.

PATRONES: Medium-sized, oval potato. Cream skin, yellow flesh. Excellent for salads. Suitable for boiling, mashing, baking, roasting and frying.

INK-EYE: Medium-sized, round potato with urple to pink colour in the eyes. White skin, ellow flesh. Most suitable for boiling, eaming, baking, roasting and salads.

SEBAGO: Medium-sized, oval potato. White skin, white flesh. Excellent for mashing. Suitable for boiling, salads, baking and roasting.

NEW POTATOES: are not a separate variety of potato, but are harvested as soon as the plant has matured, and can range from baby size to quite large. Baby new potatoes are also known as chats. They are usually cooked and served in their skins. Purchase in small amounts; use soon after purchase.

ONTIAC: Medium to large, round potato. ink-red skin, white flesh, deep eyes. Excellent r mashing. Suitable for boiling, salads, asting and baking. Not suitable for frying.

SEQUOIA: Medium to large, oval potato; large ones tend to be flattened. Smooth cream skin, white flesh. Suitable for boiling, salads, mashing, baking and roasting; not for frying.

KUMARA: sweet potatoes, including kumara, are not related to ordinary potatoes as they are not Solanum species. Shapes are long and irregular, ranging from small to large. Some species have orange skin and orange flesh, e.g., kumara (pictured above), sometimes called orange sweet potato. Other species have white flesh and skins. Sweet potatoes can be used in similar ways to potatoes, even for chipping.

ED LA SODA: Medium to large, round otato. Red skin, white flesh. Most suitable r boiling, mashing, salads, roasting and aking. Not suitable for frying.

SPUNTA: Medium to large, long potato. Cream skin, yellow flesh. Most suitable for baking, frying and dishes which use finely sliced potatoes, such as gratins.

OTHER VARIETIES
The varieties pictured are available in Australia; substitute a similar type of potato if you can't obtain these. New varieties of potatoes are constantly being developed worldwide. An example of a new potato recently introduced to Australia but not widely available is the Pink Fir Apple potato, an unusual-looking, small, long, thin potato. You may discover other varieties at your greengrocers.

USSET BURBANK: Medium to large, long otato. Rough white skin, white flesh. xcellent for frying and baking. Suitable for asting. Not suitable for salads or mashing.

TOOLANGI DELIGHT: Medium-sized, round potato. Purple skin, white flesh, deep eyes. Excellent for mashing. Suitable for boiling, baking, roasting, frying and salads.

Glossary

Here are some terms, names and alternatives to help everyone understand and use our recipes perfectly.

ARTICHOKES:
Globe: the large flower head of a plant in the thistle family.
Jerusalem: a root vegetable resembling knobbly potatoes or root ginger.

From back: Globe artichoke, Jerusalem artichokes.

BACON RASHERS: bacon slices.
BAKING POWDER: a raising agent consisting of an alkali and an acid. It is mostly made from cream of tartar and bicarbonate of soda in the proportions of 1 level teaspoon of cream of tartar to ½ level teaspoon of bicarbonate of soda. This is equivalent to 2 teaspoons of baking powder.
BEETROOT: regular round root vegetable with distinctive purple flesh; also known as beets.
BICARBONATE OF SODA: baking soda.
BREADCRUMBS:
Packaged: fine packaged breadcrumbs.
Stale: 1 or 2-day-old bread made into crumbs by grating, blending or processing.
BURGHUL (cracked wheat): wheat that is steamed until partly cooked, then dried and cracked.
BUTTER: use salted or unsalted (also called sweet) butter; 125g is equal to 1 stick butter.
BUTTERMILK: is made by adding a culture to skim milk to give a slightly acidic flavour; skim milk can be substituted, if preferred.
CAJUN BLENDED SPICE MIX: a convenient combination of dried ingredients consisting of salt, blended peppers, garlic, onion and spices.
CELERIAC: tuberous root with brown skin, white flesh and a celery-like flavour.
CHICKPEAS: garbanzos.
CHILLIES: available in many different types and sizes. Use rubber gloves when chopping fresh chillies as they can burn your skin. Keep hands away from your eyes and face.

CHORIZO SAUSAGE: spicy sausage made with pork.
COCONUT:
Milk: available from supermarkets.
COPHA: a solid white shortening based on coconut oil. Kremelta and Palmin can be substituted.
CORIANDER: also known as cilantro and Chinese parsley; available fresh, ground and in seed form. The seeds are the main ingredient of curry powder.
CORNFLOUR: cornstarch.
CORNMEAL: ground corn (maize); similar to polenta but pale yellow and finer. One can be substituted for the other, but results will vary.
COUSCOUS: a fine cereal made from semolina.
CREAM: fresh pouring cream; has a minimum fat content of 35 per cent.
Rich: also known as double cream, has a minimum fat content of 48 per cent.
Sour: a thick, commercially cultured, soured cream with 35 per cent fat content.
Thickened (whipping): has a minimum fat content of 35 per cent; it contains a thickener, such as gelatine.
CREME FRAICHE: available in cartons from delicatessens and supermarkets. To make creme fraiche, combine 300ml cream with 300ml sour cream in bowl, cover, stand at room temperature until mixture is thick; this will take 1 or 2 days, depending on the room temperature. Refrigerate before using. Makes about 2½ cups (625ml).
CURLY ENDIVE: a curly-leafed vegetable, mainly used in salads.
CURRY PASTE: we used bottled curry paste, available from supermarkets and Asian specialty stores.

Celeriac.

DILL PICKLES: pickled cucumbers.
EGG NOODLES, FRESH: made from wheat flour and eggs; varying in thickness from fine strands to pieces as thick as a shoelace.
EGGPLANT: aubergine.
ENGLISH SPINACH: a soft-leafed vegetable, more delicate in taste than silverbeet (spinach); young silverbeet can be substituted for English spinach.
ESSENCE: extract.
EYE OF LAMB LOIN: a new cut derived from the traditional loin chop. Once the bone and fat are removed, the larger portion is referred to as the eye of the loin.
FENNEL: has a slight aniseed taste when fresh, ground or in seed form. Fennel seeds are a component of curry powder. The bulb is eaten uncooked in salads or may be braised, steamed or stir-fried.

Fennel bulb.

FILLO PASTRY: also known as phyllo dough; comes in tissue-thin pastry sheets bought chilled or frozen.
FISH SAUCE: made from the liquid drained from salted, fermented anchovies. Has a strong smell and taste; use sparingly.
FLOUR:
Bread: also known as bakers' flour, has a higher protein content than plain flour, usually ranging from 12 per cent to 16 per cent. Recipes using bread flour require more kneading than plain flour.
Plain: all-purpose flour.
Potato: made from cooked potatoes which have been dried and ground.
Self-raising: substitute plain (all-purpose) flour and baking powder in the proportions of 1 cup (150g) plain flour to 2 level teaspoons baking powder. Sift together several times before using.
Wholemeal plain: wholewheat flour without the addition of baking powder.

GARAM MASALA: often used in Indian cooking, this spice combines cardamom, cinnamon, cloves, coriander, cumin and nutmeg in varying proportions. Sometimes pepper is used to make a hot variation.

GARLIC AND HERB CHEESE SPREAD: soft, spreadable processed cheese flavoured with garlic and herbs.

GHEE: a pure butter fat available in tubs and cans, it can be heated to high temperatures without burning because of the lack of salts and milk solids.

GINGER: fresh, green or root ginger: scrape away skin and grate, chop or slice as required.

GOLDEN SYRUP: maple, pancake syrup or honey can be substituted.

GRAND MARNIER: an orange-flavoured liqueur.

JALAPENO PEPPER: hot, available in brine in bottles and cans.

JAM: a preserve of sugar and fruit.

JUNIPER BERRIES: dried berries of an evergreen tree; it is the main flavouring ingredient in gin.

KUMARA: orange-coloured sweet potato; see page 121.

LARD: fat obtained from melting down and clarifying pork fat; available packaged.

LEMON GRASS: available from Asian food stores; needs to be bruised or chopped before using.

LENTILS: dried pulses. There are many different varieties, usually identified and named after their colour.

LETTUCE:
Coral: a curly-leafed lettuce.
Cos: also known as Roma; has crisp, elongated leaves.
Oak leaf: also known as Feville de Chene. Available in both red and green leaf.

Clockwise from front left: Rocket, green coral lettuce, red coral lettuce, cos lettuce, red oak leaf lettuce, curly endive, green oak leaf lettuce.

MAPLE SYRUP: we used a good quality, imported maple syrup.

MUSHROOMS:
Button: small, unopened mushrooms with a delicate flavour.
Oyster: pale grey-white mushrooms; shaped like a fan.
Shitake: used mainly in Chinese and Japanese cooking.

OIL:
Extra light/light olive: mild-tasting, light in flavour, colour and aroma, but not lower in kilojoules.
Extra virgin and virgin olive: the highest quality olive oils, obtained from the first pressings of the olives.
Olive: a blend of refined and virgin olive oils, especially good for everyday cooking.
Peanut: made from ground peanuts, this is the most commonly used oil in Asian cooking; however, a lighter salad type of oil can be used.
Sesame: an oil made from roasted, crushed white sesame seeds. Used for flavouring, not for frying.
Vegetable: we used a polyunsaturated vegetable oil.
Walnut: oil extracted from the kernel of the walnut, an expensive oil with a fine nutty flavour. Mainly used in salad dressings.

PANCETTA: cured pork belly; bacon can be substituted.

PEPPERMINT OIL: concentrated oil made from the peppermint plant. Very strong flavour, only a drop (or two) is required. Peppermint essence can be used instead.

PEPPERS: capsicum or bell peppers.

PRAWNS: shrimps.

PROSCIUTTO: uncooked, unsmoked, cured pork; ready to eat when bought.

RISONI: pasta in the shape of rice grain.

ROCKET: a green salad leaf.

SAFFRON: available in strands or ground form. The quality varies greatly.

SAMBAL OELEK (also ulek or olek): a paste made from ground chillies and salt.

SHALLOTS:
Green: also known as spring onions, scallions and eschallots.
French: very small onion with brown skin. It grows in clusters, and has a strong onion and garlic flavour.

SNOW PEAS: also known as mange tout (eat all).

SNOW PEA SPROUTS: sprouted seeds of the snow pea.

SORREL: has broad, oval-shaped leaves with a bitter, slightly sour taste.

SOUP PASTA: a combination of small mixed pasta, available in packets from health food stores.

SOY SAUCE: made from fermented soya beans.

STOCK: 1 cup (250ml) stock is the equivalent of 1 cup (250ml) water plus 1 crumbled stock cube (or 1 teaspoon stock powder). If you prefer to make your own fresh stock, see recipes on page 124.

SUGAR: we used coarse granulated table sugar, also known as crystal sugar, unless otherwise specified.
Brown: a soft, fine granulated sugar containing molasses which gives it its characteristic colour.
Caster: also known as superfine; is fine granulated table sugar.
Icing: also known as confectioners' sugar or powdered sugar. We used icing sugar mixture, not pure icing sugar, unless specified.

SUGAR SNAP PEAS: small pods with small formed peas inside; they are eaten whole, cooked or uncooked.

SWEDE: a type of turnip; also known as rutabaga.

SZECHWAN PEPPER: (also known as Chinese pepper): small, red-brown aromatic seeds resembling black peppercorns; they have a peppery-lemon flavour.

TABASCO SAUCE: made with vinegar, hot red peppers and salt. Use in drops.

TARAMA: salted, dried roe of the grey mullet fish.

TEQUILA: colourless alcoholic liquor of Mexican origin made from the fermented sap of the agave, a succulent desert plant.

TOMATO:
Canned: whole peeled tomatoes in natural juices.
Cherry tomatoes: Tom Thumb tomatoes, small and round.
Paste: a concentrated tomato puree, used in flavouring soups, stews, sauces and casseroles, etc.
Puree: canned, pureed tomatoes (not tomato paste). Use fresh, peeled, pureed tomatoes as a substitute, if preferred.
Sauce: tomato ketchup.
Sun-dried: dried tomatoes. We use dried tomatoes that are bottled in oil, unless otherwise specified.
Supreme: a canned product consisting of tomatoes, onions, celery, peppers and seasonings.

TORTILLA: thin, round, unleavened bread; can be bought or made at home. Recipes for flour tortillas and corn tortillas are given in our *Easy Mexican-Style Cookery* cookbook.

TURMERIC: a member of the ginger family, its root is ground and dried, giving the rich yellow powder which gives curry its characteristic colour; it is not hot in flavour.

VINEGAR: we used both white and brown malt vinegar.
Balsamic: originated in the province of Modena, Italy. Regional wine is specially processed then aged in antique wooden casks to give a pungent flavour.
Cider: vinegar made from fermented apples.
Red wine: is based on red wine.
White: made from spirit of cane sugar.

WATER CHESTNUTS: small, white, crisp bulbs with brown skin. Canned water chestnuts are peeled and will keep for about a month in the refrigerator covered with their brine.

WILD RICE: from North America, but not a member of the rice family. It is expensive as it is difficult to cultivate but has a distinctive flavour.

YEAST: allow 2 teaspoons (7g) dried yeast to each 15g compressed yeast if substituting one for the other.

ZUCCHINI: courgette.

MAKE YOUR OWN STOCK

BEEF STOCK
2kg meaty beef bones
2 medium (300g) onions
2 sticks celery, chopped
2 medium (250g) carrots, chopped
3 bay leaves
2 teaspoons black peppercorns
5 litres (20 cups) water
3 litres (12 cups) water, extra
Place bones and unpeeled chopped onions in baking dish. Bake in hot oven about 1 hour or until bones and onions are well browned. Transfer bones and onions to large pan, add celery, carrots, bay leaves, peppercorns and water, simmer, uncovered, 3 hours. Add extra water, simmer, uncovered, further 1 hour; strain.
Makes about 2.5 litres (10 cups).
- Stock can be made 4 days ahead.
- Storage: Covered, in refrigerator.
- Freeze: Suitable.
- Microwave: Not suitable.

CHICKEN STOCK
2kg chicken bones
2 medium (300g) onions, chopped
2 sticks celery, chopped
2 medium (250g) carrots, chopped
3 bay leaves
2 teaspoons black peppercorns
5 litres (20 cups) water
Combine all ingredients in large pan, simmer, uncovered, 2 hours; strain.
Makes about 2.5 litres (10 cups).
- Stock can be made 4 days ahead.
- Storage: Covered, in refrigerator.
- Freeze: Suitable.
- Microwave: Not suitable.

FISH STOCK
1.5kg fish bones
3 litres (12 cups) water
1 medium (150g) onion, chopped
2 sticks celery, chopped
2 bay leaves
1 teaspoon black peppercorns

Combine all ingredients in large pan, simmer, uncovered, 20 minutes; strain.
Makes about 2.5 litres (10 cups).
- Stock can be made 4 days ahead.
- Storage: Covered, in refrigerator.
- Freeze: Suitable.
- Microwave: Not suitable.

VEGETABLE STOCK
1 large (180g) carrot, chopped
1 large (180g) parsnip, chopped
2 medium (300g) onions, chopped
6 sticks celery, chopped
4 bay leaves
2 teaspoons black peppercorns
3 litres (12 cups) water
Combine all ingredients in large pan, simmer, uncovered, 1½ hours; strain.
Makes about 1.25 litres (5 cups).
- Stock can be made 4 days ahead.
- Storage: Covered, in refrigerator.
- Freeze: Suitable.
- Microwave: Suitable.

Index

QUICK CONVERSION GUIDE

Wherever you live in the world you can use our recipes with the help of our easy-to-follow conversions for all your cooking needs. These conversions are approximate only. The difference between the exact and approximate conversions of liquid and dry measures amounts to only a teaspoon or two, and will not make any difference to your cooking results.

MEASURING EQUIPMENT

The difference between measuring cups internationally is minimal within 2 or 3 teaspoons' difference. (For the record, 1 Australian metric measuring cup will hold approximately 250ml.) The most accurate way of measuring dry ingredients is to weigh them. When measuring liquids use a clear glass or plastic jug with metric markings.

If you would like the measuring cups and spoons as used in our Test Kitchen, turn to page 128 for details and order coupon. In this book we use metric measuring cups and spoons approved by Standards Australia.

● a graduated set of four cups for measuring dry ingredients; the sizes are marked on the cups.
● a graduated set of four spoons for measuring dry and liquid ingredients; the amounts are marked on the spoons.
● 1 TEASPOON: 5ml.
● 1 TABLESPOON: 20ml.

NOTE: NZ, CANADA, USA AND UK ALL USE 15ml TABLESPOONS.
ALL CUP AND SPOON MEASUREMENTS ARE LEVEL.

DRY MEASURES

METRIC	IMPERIAL
15g	½oz
30g	1oz
60g	2oz
90g	3oz
125g	4oz (¼lb)
155g	5oz
185g	6oz
220g	7oz
250g	8oz (½lb)
280g	9oz
315g	10oz
345g	11oz
375g	12oz (¾lb)
410g	13oz
440g	14oz
470g	15oz
500g	16oz (1lb)
750g	24oz (1½lb)
1kg	32oz (2lb)

LIQUID MEASURES

METRIC	IMPERIAL
30ml	1 fluid oz
60ml	2 fluid oz
100ml	3 fluid oz
125ml	4 fluid oz
150ml	5 fluid oz (¼ pint/1 gill)
190ml	6 fluid oz
250ml	8 fluid oz
300ml	10 fluid oz (½ pint)
500ml	16 fluid oz
600ml	20 fluid oz (1 pint)
1000ml (1 litre)	1¾ pints

**WE USE LARGE EGGS
WITH AN AVERAGE
WEIGHT OF 60g**

HELPFUL MEASURES

METRIC	IMPERIAL
3mm	⅛in
6mm	¼in
1cm	½in
2cm	¾in
2.5cm	1in
5cm	2in
6cm	2½in
8cm	3in
10cm	4in
13cm	5in
15cm	6in
18cm	7in
20cm	8in
23cm	9in
25cm	10in
28cm	11in
30cm	12in (1ft)

HOW TO MEASURE

When using the graduated metric measuring cups, it is important to shake the dry ingredients loosely into the required cup. Do not tap the cup on the bench, or pack the ingredients into the cup unless otherwise directed. Level top of cup with knife. When using graduated metric measuring spoons, level top of spoon with knife. When measuring liquids in the jug, place jug on flat surface, check for accuracy at eye level.

OVEN TEMPERATURES

These oven temperatures are only a guide; we've given you the lower degree of heat. Always check the manufacturer's manual.

	C° (Celsius)	F° (Fahrenheit)	Gas Mark
Very slow	120	250	1
Slow	150	300	2
Moderately slow	160	325	3
Moderate	180 – 190	350 – 375	4
Moderately hot	200 – 210	400 – 425	5
Hot	220 – 230	450 – 475	6
Very hot	240 – 250	500 – 525	7

TWO GREAT OFFERS FROM THE AWW HOME LIBRARY

Here's the perfect way to keep your Home Library books in order, clean and within easy reach. More than a dozen books fit into this smart silver grey vinyl folder. PRICE: Australia $11.95; elsewhere $21.95; prices include postage and handling. To order your holder, see the details below.

All recipes in the AWW Home Library are created using Australia's unique system of metric cups and spoons. While it is relatively easy for overseas readers to make any minor conversions required, it is easier still to own this durable set of Australian cups and spoons (photographed). PRICE : Australia: $5.95; New Zealand: $A8.00; elsewhere: $A9.95; prices include postage & handling.
This offer is available in all countries.

TO ORDER YOUR METRIC MEASURING SET OR BOOK HOLDER:

PHONE: Have your credit card details ready. **Sydney:** (02) 260 0035; **elsewhere in Australia:** 008 252 515 (free call, Mon-Fri, 9am-5pm) or *FAX* your order to (02) 267 4363 or *MAIL* your order by photocopying or cutting out and completing the coupon below.

PAYMENT: **Australian residents:** We accept the credit cards listed, money orders and cheques. **Overseas residents:** We accept the credit cards listed, drafts in $A drawn on an Australian bank, also English, New Zealand and U.S. cheques in the currency of the country of issue.
Credit card charges are at the exchange rate current at the time of payment.

Please photocopy and complete coupon and fax or send to:
AWW Home Library Reader Offer, ACP Direct, PO Box 7036, Sydney 2001.

❏ Metric Measuring Set   ❏ Holder
Please indicate number(s) required.
Mr/Mrs/Ms _____
Address _____
_____
Postcode _____ Country _____
Ph: (   ) _____ Bus. Hour: _____
I enclose my cheque/money order for $ _____ payable to ACP Direct

OR: please charge my:
❏ Bankcard ❏ Visa ❏ MasterCard ❏ Diners Club ❏ Amex
❏❏❏❏❏❏❏❏❏❏❏❏❏❏❏❏ Exp. Date ___/__
Cardholder's signature_____

(Please allow up to 30 days for delivery within Australia. Allow up to 6 weeks for overseas deliveries.)
Both offers expire 30/12/95.   AWSF95